HEALTHY MICROWAVE COOKING

HEALTHY MICROWAVE COOKING

by Judith Benn Hurley

BETTER NUTRITION
IN HALF THE TIME!

Photography by The Rodale Press Photography Department

RODALE PRESS, EMMAUS, PA.

Printed in the United States of America on recycled paper
containing a high percentage of de-inked fiber.

Illustrations Copyright © 1988 by Janet Bohn

Recipe photograph on front cover: Marinated Stuffed Beef
(Matambre), page 184. Recipe photographs on back cover:
Shrimp in a Bamboo Steamer, page 134; Dessert Crepes,
page 241; Tiny Whole Carrots with Mustard and Chervil,
page 85.

Plates, glassware and linens in photographs courtesy of
Appel-Jeweler, Inc., Allentown, Pa.

Library of Congress Cataloging-in-Publication Data

Hurley, Judith Benn.
    Healthy microwave cooking : better nutrition in half the
time! / by Judith Benn Hurley ; photography by the Rodale
Press Photography Department.
        p.   cm.
    Includes index.
    ISBN 0–87857–771–8
    1. Microwave cookery.   I. Title.
TX832.H87   1988
641.5′882–dc 19   88–11329
                                                                     CIP

2   4   6   8   10   9   7   5   3   1   hardcover

To my Pat,
for your love
and hearty appetite

CONTENTS

ACKNOWLEDGMENTS

Cheers and thanks to:

JoAnn Brader, who supervised recipe testing with her unfailing expertise.

Beth A. Pianucci and Nancy J. Zelko for research.

Stauffer's Seafood, Weaver's Orchard, Ulrich's Produce, Neidermyer Poultry, Pathmark, Balthaser's Meats, By the Scoop, Wilcox Roadside Market, The Mail Room and Monoson, who helped to bring me inspiration in Reading, Pennsylvania.

Rubbermaid, Litton, Regal Ware, Inc., Northland Aluminum Products, Inc., Republic Molding Corp., Eagle Affiliates, J. G. Durand Int., Farberware, Anchor Hocking Corp. and H. P. Mayer for giving me the opportunity to explore their products.

Antoinette and Bruce and Gail and Tom for frequently inviting me to dinner.

Special thanks to my editors, Charlie Gerras, Camille Bucci and Debora Tkac. Their support and wisdom has, once again, made me a very lucky author.

INTRODUCTION— THE NEW WAVE IN COOKING

Many cooks still regard microwave cooking as artless and unrefined. To them, microwaving means only reheating institutional and convenience foods. Blame it on the many microwave cookbooks that contain recipes and concepts that could heave the gastronomic revolution back three decades. They are dull, pursue pre-prepared ingredients and are often just plain tacky.

Healthy Microwave Cooking is different. It offers a fresh, healthful approach to microwaving through delicious, imaginative recipes. An especially innovative aspect of this book is that it presents an honest look at microwaving. You'll learn which foods work well in a microwave and, perhaps more important, you'll learn which don't.

When Is an Oven Not an Oven?

When it's a microwave. Repeat after me: "The microwave is not an oven. It is a kitchen accessory." Learn this lesson well. Do not expect your microwave to perform like a conventional oven, but faster. It won't.

So what can a microwave do? A fabulous job on high water content, low-fat foods like fish, poultry, vegetables and fruits. They microwave deliciously and can offer outstanding health benefits.

Microwaves cook with moist heat and there's no hot air to evaporate the steam. This means that browning is very, very limited, so forget about roasting or broiling.

Forget about microwaving breads, soufflés, cakes, roast meats and pie crusts. And if you like a crisp-skinned baked potato, bake it in a conventional oven because your microwave won't do the job.

Also remember that a great microwave benefit is speed and that microwaving large amounts of food at one time defeats that benefit. Why? Because the same number of waves are present whether you're microwaving one or one dozen pieces of chicken: More food means fewer waves per item, hence longer cooking time.

The same goes for huge hunks of food. Since the waves can only penetrate the first 2 inches of food, the insides of large pieces must cook by conduction. Depending on what's being cooked, this can leave tough outsides and/or raw insides. Remember this when you're considering microwaving your Thanksgiving turkey.

Microwave Cooking Is Healthful Cooking

Next to the weather, health is probably the subject people talk about most. It's on everyone's mind. Concern with fat intake as it relates to healthy hearts attracts many people to microwaving. It's a perfect low-fat cooking method that enhances the flavor of fresh foods while keeping them moist.

Through its speed, microwaving also preserves vitamins and minerals. Keep in mind that loss of nutrients begins the second cooking begins: The shorter the cooking time, the fewer nutrients lost. Combine this with my fresh-ingredient recommendations and you're way ahead in the health race.

Healthy Microwave Cooking offers salt-free recipes, partially because salting food prior to microwaving tends to dry it out. You'll find there's no need to salt after cooking either, because the recipes in this book are creatively seasoned and tasty.

Really Good Recipes

"Some foods can't be cooked well in it," is the most common complaint of microwave owners. This book offers only recipes that are appropriate for microwaving. And to make the cook's life even easier they require few preparation steps.

I provide recipes that accommodate today's hectic pace and, at the same time, offer interesting, healthful alternatives to fatty convenience foods. You'll discover microwaving with lean, fresh fish and seafood; beautiful garden vegetables; plump, skinless poultry and a treasury of herbs and spices. You'll also discover how easy it is to microwave without excessive saturated fats.

If you're eager to explore delicious, beautiful and healthful microwave foods, this is the book that lets you do it with ease and style.

HOW THIS BOOK CAN HELP YOU STAY HEALTHY

When I stoke up the grill to create new recipes, I think of aromatic foods. Stir-frying makes me focus on the colors and textures of food. But when microwaving, whether it's a rich chunk of salmon or fragrant squash bâtons, I think of good health. Why boil beautiful baby potatoes when you can toss them into the microwave to cook and preserve nutrients as well as flavors and textures? Why fry plump, tender chicken when microwaving will make it succulent without added fat or calories?

I'm sure you get the idea. The recipes and cooking techniques in *Healthy Microwave Cooking* were designed to bring out the best in nutritious foods so they don't need adornment from health-robbing ingredients. Clams with Cucumber-Leek Sauce, for instance, adopts bold leeks, silky cukes and fragrant herbs to show off the fresh clams: No butter necessary.

For you, all this may be a new way to cook. But we all keep hearing about "eating light" and *Healthy Microwave Cooking* shows you the tasty, convenient way to do it. The techniques are a snap, the recipes are delicious and, best of all, they can help keep you healthy.

One way to begin is to think about what you're eating now and how you can replace it easily with recipes from this book. See the list on the next page. If your eating habits match the foods in the left column, start preparing the ones on the right, instead.

Traditional Food	Healthy Microwave Cooking
Deep-fried wontons	Crisp Wonton Fans (page 35)
Salty soup stock	Chicken Stock (page 46)
Fatty sausages	Seafood Sausage with Avocado Cream (page 127)
Deep-fried shrimp	Shrimp in a Bamboo Steamer (page 134)
Fried chicken	Mustard-Poached Chicken with Zucchini Relish (page 153)
Fatty coffee cake	Apricot Snack Bars (page 237)
Fatty pancakes	Dessert Crepes (page 241)
Sugary breakfast cereal	Raisin-Oat Granola (page 249)

You're probably wondering exactly how *Healthy Microwave Cooking* can help you stay healthy. You'll see in my recipes that many of the advantages of microwave cooking conveniently overlap—you can help keep your heart healthy, regulate your cholesterol, guard against cancer and stay trim all at the same time.

Heart-Healthy Foods

It's no secret that cutting fat from the diet is a real favor you can do for your heart. Now you can prepare lean fish and poultry with little or no added fat because microwaving leaves them moist and juicy automatically.

- If fat's bad for a healthy heart, then deep frying is the ultimate bad deed. I will teach you how to prepare such classics as wontons and crisp tortilla chips without going near the deep fryer.
- Potassium, which is essential to a healthy heart, is abundant in dried apricots. Use your microwave to quickly plump them, then add to fruit

compotes, yogurt or hot breakfast cereals. Acorn squash and white potatoes (plus skins) are also high in potassium. Thanks to microwaving, you can prepare these heart-healthy vegetables in a flash on busy weeknights.

- Omega-3 fatty acids can help reduce harmful cholesterol levels and triglycerides plus help keep your arteries clear. The best source of omega-3s is fish, and research suggests that just three fish meals a week might make a healthful difference. Lucky for us, fish is delicious and moist when microwaved, even without added fat. Note that sardines, salmon, mackerel, fresh tuna and rainbow trout are fish high in omega-3s.
- Oat bran, which can also help lower excessive cholesterol counts, can be easily microwaved for a healthful breakfast. For fast results, use a 9-inch (23-cm) glass pie dish instead of the one recommended on the box.
- Olive oil, yet another means of cholesterol control, becomes deliciously fruity when microwaved. It's also nice when tossed with just-microwaved broccoli or zucchini and fresh crushed thyme or basil.
- Research proposes that adding pectin to the diet can reduce harmful levels of cholesterol. Soybeans are high in pectin and microwaving can speed their cooking. Grapefruit is also high in pectin—if you warm a half in the microwave before eating, its flavors will emerge and you won't need any sweetener.

Lean Living

We already know that microwaving is low-fat or no-fat cooking, so use your imagination to cut calories.

- Instead of sautéing those chopped onions in fat, microwave them.

- If you're counting calories (and watching your cholesterol, for that matter), you should be cutting down on saturated fat in your diet. Beef, usually high in saturated fat, can be successfully microwaved so that much of the fat will actually melt away.
- High-fiber fruit is nutritious and keeps you feeling fuller longer. So microwave a whole apple with honey and nuts for dessert instead of reaching for that apple pie.
- Several studies suggest that people who eat hot soup at a meal consume fewer calories than those who don't. Microwaving helps you prepare nutritious soups speedily and reheat individual portions in no time.
- Granola baked in a conventional oven may require ½ cup (120 ml) of oil for each 2½ cups (600 ml) of grain to keep from burning. Microwaved granola (with the same amount of grain) needs a mere 2 teaspoons (10 ml) of oil.
- Cheese, which is important to our health for the calcium it supplies, is often high in fat and calories. *Healthy Microwave Cooking* shows you how to make your own no-fat-added cream cheese in the microwave in less than five minutes.
- Low-fat fruit butters and fruit sauces are easy to prepare in the microwave. They make great low-calorie desserts because microwaving leaves the fruit sweet and fragrant with no need to add fats and sugars.

A Flair for Fiber

High-fiber diets have been associated with lowered rates of heart disease, various cancers and obesity. Microwaving can help put more fiber in your diet by making it easier for you to prepare high-fiber foods. Beans, cracked wheat, high-fiber hot cereals and high-fiber vegetables are often long-cooking foods. But microwaving makes them accessible to even the busiest of cooks. And if you're a pasta fan, you'll be pleased to know that I offer great sauces in this book to top it off.

Slash Sodium

Low-sodium diets have been linked with lowering blood pressure and aiding weight loss. There's not a grain of added salt in my recipes and I include recipes for a no-salt-added cheese and pâté. Instead of salt, lively combinations of herbs and aromatics are used to enhance flavor. Also note that food to be microwaved should never be salted anyway because the salt will dry it out.

Hang On to Valuable Vitamins

Research suggests that vitamin C can help slow down the deterioration of our arterial walls, fight colds, cancer and infections, and even help us absorb iron. The problem is, vitamin C is heat sensitive and water soluble, which means that most cooking methods rob much of it from our food. Microwaving actually helps retain vitamin C because of its speed and minimal water requirements. Thiamine, which is important to our digestion and nervous system, is also preserved by microwaving as are riboflavin and niacin, which help our bodies assimilate nutrients from the food we eat.

Anticancer Body Guards

The American Cancer Society advises that we eat fewer processed foods and more "real" foods. They also suggest that a diet high in cruciferous vegetables (members of the mustard family), especially cabbage, broccoli, Brussels sprouts, dark leafy greens and spinach, can actually help defend our bodies against cancer. These are made-for-microwave vegetables. They require a minimum of water and a short cooking time so color, flavor and nutrients are retained.

More health tips are included in the introductions that precede the recipe chapters and with the recipes themselves.

How the Recipes Measure Up

On each side of the list of ingredients in a recipe you'll find a number: The left side gives U.S. measurement. The right side gives metric units, the measure used overseas. One side may be unfamiliar to you, depending on which side of the ocean you do your cooking.

If you are familiar with both sides, however, you'll notice that my conversions are not exact. For example, a liter does not equal a quart; it equals a quart *plus* a quarter cup. Neither does a pound exactly equal 450 grams nor a ¼ cup equal 60 milliliters. But they're close—avoiding the problem of having to use eyedroppers and decimal points!—and they follow the equivalents generally used in recipe translation.

If you are unfamiliar with metric conversion, the following will give you an idea of what you'll find in the recipes in *Healthy Microwave Cooking*.

U.S.	Metric
1 teaspoon (tsp)	5 milliliters (ml)
1 tablespoon (Tbs)	15 milliliters (ml)
1 cup	240 milliliters (ml)
1 pound (lb)	450 grams (g)

MICROWAVE FUNDAMENTALS

Notes on Microwave Cooking Times

Cooks new to microwaving sometimes find the timing confusing. If you are one of these, the tips that follow will help put you on the right track.

- Cooking times in recipes will guide you, but results will vary depending on the size, shape and wattage of the microwave oven you're using. So when a time range is given, start checking for doneness with the shortest time given.
- At peak electric load times (dinnertime is one) your microwave may put out less power than usual. This is called a voltage drop and can also happen if a microwave is plugged into the same circuit as another large appliance in use, like a refrigerator. Also, make sure your microwave is plugged into an outlet in accordance with manufacturer's instructions.
- Cold food will take longer to microwave than room temperature food.
- Microwaving in a dish that's too large for the amount of food will increase cooking time.
- Loose covers like crumpled waxed paper and paper towels will increase cooking time. Tight covers, like vented plastic wrap or a snug lid, will cut cooking time down.
- The recipes in this book were created in a 700 watt microwave. If your microwave has a different

Cooking Time Chart

Watts	Cooking Time									
700	1:00	2:00	3:00	4:00	5:00	6:00	7:00	8:00	9:00	10:00
650	1:11	2:22	3:33	4:44	5:55	7:06	8:17	9:28	10:39	11:50
600	1:14	2:28	3:42	4:56	6:10	7:24	8:38	9:52	11:06	12:20
550	1:17	2:34	3:51	5:08	6:25	7:42	8:59	10:16	11:33	12:50
500	1:20	2:40	4:00	5:20	6:40	8:00	9:20	10:40	12:00	13:20

wattage, use the Cooking Time Chart above to find the timing. Microwaves that have under 500 watts of power should be used for reheating only.

Microwave Cookware: What You Really Need

This is tricky. It's like telling you what car to buy, and that's largely a matter of personal taste. If you're excited in some way by a piece of cookware, you'll be a better and more imaginative cook when you use it.

Here are some guidelines to consider.

- Circular and flat is the best shape for even, efficient microwaving.
- If you like to participate with the food you cook, microwaving may be frustrating because you can't really touch or smell it. But if you use see-through cookware, at least you can see it.
- Some plastic-type materials don't let foods cook as fast as glass does, but the plastic types seem to hold heat better than glass.
- Some plastic-type cookware stains easily from the foods cooked in it. Potatoes with skins and blueberries are big culprits. If you experience staining on your cookware, make a paste of

baking soda and lemon juice and rub it into the surface. Cover with a damp paper towel and let it sit for a while. Then wash.

- A temperature probe should not be used for large, unskinned poultry and fatty roasts because dripping fat may cause a false reading, as can irregular shapes and bones. The best use for a probe is for reheating foods, like casseroles, and then you want the temperature to be 150°F (66°C).

- An instant-read microwave thermometer is handy to check the internal temperature of pork, which should be 170°F (77°C).

- If your microwave has a shelf that allows you to cook two things at once, remember that the top dish could shield the bottom one from cooking. So if you use the shelf, rotate the top and bottom dishes during cooking.

Selecting a Set

The majority of microwave cookware is for reheating, the best of which can go from freezer or refrigerator to table (lids included). Many of these containers do a good job of keeping food hot for a long time after microwaving.

If you buy a set of cookware, make sure all the pieces will fit into your microwave, especially if it's a compact one. It's also nice if the pieces nest, for easy storage.

Also be sure the roasting rack is well slotted so that air can circulate underneath the food.

Browning Dish Basics

A browning dish won't really brown food. In fact, the dish itself can get brown if you don't handle it carefully. For instance, after preheating you may want to paint on a bit of oil. Peanut or olive oil can be used. But vegetable cooking spray will turn brown.

In any case, browning dishes do alter the texture of food by sort of searing the food enough to make you notice it has not been poached or stewed. Therefore, they can be worthwhile.

Most browning dishes retain food odors. And unless you don't mind your chicken tasting like last night's fish, this can be a problem. One way to help remove odors is to make a paste of baking soda and lemon juice and rub it over the surface of the dish. Cover with a wet paper towel and let it soak for about an hour. Then wash.

There are two basic surfaces—nonstick and regular. The nonstick surface, like the sauté pan you use on a burner, is easy to clean and can help you reduce fat and calories from your diet. On the other hand, browning dishes with regular surfaces heat faster and do a better job searing the surface of the food. The choice may depend on what surface you're used to in conventional cooking. You may even want both.

Regardless of surface, look for a browning dish with gutters around the perimeter. They'll catch fat and juices while the food is cooking.

Some browning dishes come with a domed cover. These covers shouldn't be used for actual cooking because they tend to promote a steaming action, rather than browning. They are, however, nice for keeping food warm after it's been cooked. If you want to avoid splattering, don't use a cover; loosely shield the food with crumpled waxed paper.

Also note that, unlike other microwave cookware, the shape of the browning dish has no effect on even cooking. Round, square or rectangular are all the same.

Turntable Tips

If your microwave doesn't have its own turntable, you can buy one, and it will automatically rotate cooking dishes so that you don't have to do it. You will, however, have to stop it and stir the food, because the food in the middle isn't really changing position.

Turntables will hold from 8 to 10 pounds (4 to 5 kg) and will automatically rotate for 20 to 30 minutes. Some are nonstick, which is a handy feature, and others are dishwasher-safe, which is handy, too. One type even has little guides to help you position food correctly. Choose to suit your needs and measure first to be sure the turntable will fit in your microwave.

Egg Cookers

These are usually round with little cups in which to cook shelled eggs. Nonstick surfaces are the easiest to use and also do a great job on tiny custards and timbales.

In one kind of cooker you can actually cook eggs in their shells. The process takes a bit longer than conventional cooking but the device is easy to handle and the eggs come out even and delicious.

Popcorn Poppers

You won't save time by microwaving popcorn, but you don't need oil so you will save fat and calories. The best kinds of microwave poppers are cone shaped with a wide top and a very narrow bottom. That, plus a sturdy, heat-attracting material, helps kernels pop.

Many microwave popcorn poppers come with inserts that allow them to double as steamers, which is a nice touch.

Special Utensils

Microwave utensils have handles that are bent at the elbows to help you stir and flip food easily and safely while it's still in the microwave. The choices are a whisk, spatula, large spoon and ladle.

Wrapping It Up

Plastic wrap, waxed paper and paper towels are all useful, efficient and very different in the results they produce. These guidelines will make you an expert in no time, and soon you'll be inventing your own ways to use each.

Plastic Wrap

This is the covering that provides maximum steam and moisture. It's perfect with foods that could dry out, like chicken cutlets and delicate fish fillets, and also with foods like soups and stews that need to be simmered. Plastic wrap is a very tight cover, so it's great for keeping vegetables moist without a lot of added fat or water. Husked and rinsed corn on the cob, for example, will remain moist and juicy when wrapped individually in plastic wrap and microwaved.

Plastic wrap is the covering you'll probably use the most, and should always be vented when used to cover a dish. To vent, simply leave a 1-inch (2.5-cm) slit open along the edge where the plastic wrap meets the dish. Venting allows a bit of steam to escape and will keep the plastic wrap from splitting during microwaving.

Plastic wrap is easiest to remove after standing time, but if the food's still steamy, be sure to open away from your face.

Waxed Paper

Use waxed paper when you want to hold heat but let some moisture escape. In other words, use it when you don't want foods to appear steamed. Half of a winter squash, spaghetti squash or eggplant, when wrapped in waxed paper, will microwave firmer than if you use plastic wrap. The firmer texture makes them easier to stuff or grill.

Use waxed paper to prevent juicy foods, like tomato sauce, from splattering and to line steamers so tiny foods, like bay scallops, won't fall through. Use it for the dry microwaving of foods that stick, like fish fillets and granola, and use it crumpled to prevent tiny things, like seeds, from hopping out of the dish.

Note that if your microwave has a strong fan, you may need to tuck the waxed paper under a dish or some heavy foods so it doesn't blow around.

Paper Towels

If you want dry or crisp results, use dry paper towels. Wontons, tortilla chips, grated coconut and bread crumbs are good examples of foods that work well because the towel absorbs their moisture. Try to avoid microwaving fish on paper towels because it can stick and be difficult to remove.

If you want a bit more moisture but maximum air circulation, use a damp paper towel. Flour tortillas wrapped in a damp paper towel emerge warm and neither dry nor soggy. To warm sandwiches and frozen muffins, use this technique.

Be sure to use only white paper towels because colored ones could bleed on food.

MAKING MENUS MEANINGFUL

It's my hope that you'll feel comfortable enough to blend the recipes in this book into your regular culinary routine. You may see a vegetable recipe that will enhance a favorite chicken dish, or a delicious dessert to end the perfect evening.

Still, since so many of the recipes in *Healthy Microwave Cooking* combine together to make interesting meals, I'm compelled to make a few suggestions.

Light Night

For bikini season.

    Asparagus with Thyme and Orange Butter
    Sea Salad with Lemon and Watercress
    Fruit with Creamy Grape Dressing

Double Happiness

This type of Chinese meal is also referred to as Double Mouthful because it promises two benefits: good taste and good health.

    Wontons Filled with Rice and Chives
    Egg Flower Soup
    Chinese Vegetables with Sesame Garnish
    Shrimp with Two Fragrant Sauces
    Glazed Fresh Peaches with Apricot Preserve

Fast and Delicious

When your relatives show up without calling first.

    Tiny Whole Carrots with Mustard and Chervil
    Sliced Beef Salad with Potato Bâtons
    Orange-Almond Custard

At the Casbah

An oasis in your day.

    Stuffed Grape Leaves
    Circassian Chicken
        or
    Roasted meat with Garlic Chili Sauce
       (Harissa)
    Almond Fruit Bars

Hot Summer's Night

Stay cool with this menu.

    Garlic Puree with Ricotta (with crudités)
    Salmon Trout with Mustard and Dill
    Creamy Peach Soup

Hunter's Dinner

Robust and hearty.

    Swiss Fondue *(Raclette)*
    Beef with Winter Vegetables
    Puree of Winter Squash with Rosemary
    Apples or Pears with Caramel Sauce

Candlelight Dinner

Send the kids to the movies.

    Shrimp and Smoked Salmon Bisque
    Black Bass in Parchment
    Stuffed artichokes
    Cheesecake Mousse with Raspberry-Lemon Glaze

Southeast Asian Buffet

From Thailand, Malaysia, Indonesia, Laos and Korea.
Great for a party.

Scallops with Green Curry Sauce
Fresh Egg Rolls
Fragrant Mussels
Hot and Sour Shrimp with Crunchy Lettuce
Korean Sesame Beef
In Banana Heaven

Fiesta!

¡Con mucho gusto!

Tortilla chips
Jicama Bâtons with Cumin and Lime
Red Snapper with Jalapeño Butter
   or
Soft Tortillas with *Piccadillo* Filling
Pumpkin Custard

Waffle Bar

Here's another idea for brunch. Bake the waffles as
usual, in a waffle iron. Then set them into a 200°F
(94°C) oven, right on the oven racks, to keep them
warm. When you're ready, serve with:

Blueberry-Orange *Coulis*
Creamy Grape Dressing
Strawberry-Pear Puree
Maple Vanilla Ice Cream (or Ice Milk)

Sunday Dinner at Miss Lucille's

A country menu.

Honey Chicken on Rice
Brussels sprouts
Louisiana Broil with Cajun Hot Sauce
Peach Bread Pudding with Pecans

Little Pleasures from India
Fragrant and exotic.
> Toasted pumpkin seeds
> Chick-Pea and Potato Curry
> East Indian Barbecue Seasoning (*Tikka* Paste)
>   over flounder
> Rice Pudding with Cardamom and Almonds

Livio's Choice
Favorites of a great Italian chef.
> Favas, Italian Style
> Chicken Scallopini with Tomato Butter and Ziti
> Braised Fennel with Parmesan and Ripe Tomatoes
> Dried Fruit Compote

The Perfect Picnic
Find a shady spot near a clear, bubbling brook.
> Quick Tomato and Feta Sandwiches
> Shrimp with Garlic-Almond Pesto
> Maple Vanilla Ice Cream (or Ice Milk)
> Apricot Snack Bars

Bravo for Brunch!
This menu works for both buffet and sit-down meals.
> Garlic Soup Gratiné
> Cherry Tomato Cocktail
> Corn Cake with Ricotta and Pimientos
> Frozen Lime and Honey Mousse

American Bistro
Casual chic.
> Marinated Chevre with Rosemary and Garlic
> Mustard-Poached Chicken with Zucchini Relish
> Ragout of Wild Mushrooms
> Pear Fans in Mango Puree

Japanese Buffet

A delicious and interesting menu for entertaining.

Lemon Miso Soup with Vegetable Julienne and
   Skinny Noodles
Japanese Eggplant Salad
Picnic Chicken from Japan
Beef with Garlic Sauce
Warm Citrus Compote

Best of Brazil

South American food that's simple and savory.

Shrimp from Rio
Sweet Potato Salad with Peanut Dressing
Marinated Stuffed Beef *(Matambre)*
Pears and Plantains

MICROWAVE
IN MINUTES

I t's never easy to determine the exact time it will take to prepare a recipe. I may chop faster than you. You may have extra help in the kitchen. Some cooks may even use convenience items like prepared garlic (and shame on them if they do). But however you work in your kitchen, I'm pleased to report that about half the recipes in *Healthy Microwave Cooking* take well under 20 minutes to prepare. Simple, fresh ingredients are the secret.

For your convenience, the following list divides these speedy recipes by chapter heading.

15 Minutes or Under

The Healthier Happy Hour
Escargots with Shallot Butter
Snow Peas with Two Dipping Sauces
Mushroom Caps with Pecans and Basil
Artichokes
Ragout of Wild Mushrooms
Tortilla chips
Crisp Wonton Fans
Wontons Filled with Rice and Chives
Eggplant Dunk with Garlic Studs

Sensational Soups
Japanese Fish Stock *(Dashi)*
Clear Broth with See-Through Wontons

Egg Flower Soup
Sweet Potato Vichyssoise
Tomato Soup with Tuna and Fresh Basil
Spring Rendezvous
Garlic Soup Gratiné
Carrot Soup with Roots and Tops
Broccoli Puree with Fennel and Parmesan
Cowboy Soup
Lemon Miso Soup with Vegetable Julienne and
    Skinny Noodles

From the Garden
Sweet Potato Salad with Peanut Dressing
Chinese Vegetables with Sesame Garnish
Onions in a Bag
Braised Fennel with Parmesan and Ripe Tomatoes
Tiny Whole Carrots with Mustard and Chervil
Jicama Bâtons with Cumin and Lime
Garlic Puree with Ricotta
Butternut Squash with Cider Cream
Marinated Sweet Peppers
Asparagus with Thyme and Orange Butter
Butterflied Eggplant with Garlic and Olive Oil
Baby Pattypans with Balsamic Vinaigrette

From Rivers and Seas
Dill Butter
Shark Steak with Fennel Aioli
Scallops with Dried Tomatoes
Black Bass in Parchment
Sea Salad with Lemon and Watercress
Shrimp with Two Fragrant Sauces
Poached Fresh Tuna with Aromatics
Orange Roughy with Tomato, Lemon and Mint
Hot and Sour Shrimp with Crunchy Lettuce
East Indian Barbecue Seasoning (*Tikka* Paste)

Birds of a Feather
Fricassee of Chicken with Fresh Basil
Chicken Oregano with Spaghetti
Hot Pepper Butter
Chicken with Cashews and Broccoli
Chicken with Apricots and Rosemary
Thai Glaze
Terrines of Chicken with Leeks
Chicken with Dried Tomatoes and Tiny Pasta
Chicken with Grapefruit

New Wave Meats
Skewered Beef in Peanut Sauce
Garlic Chili Sauce *(Harissa)*
Mustard Sauce
Beef with Garlic Sauce
Savannah Barbecue Sauce
Horseradish Cream
Veal with Dried Tomatoes and Mozzarella
Veal with Citrus and Sage
Tangy Fruit Glaze
Lamb with Garlic and Lemon

Enlightened Entrées
Crisp Tortillas with Black Beans and Yams
Vegetable Frittata Arles
Savory Mexican Pie *(Chilaquiles)*
Stuffed Sweet Peppers with Fresh Tomato Sauce
Quick Cracked Wheat
Spaghetti Squash
Sichuan Noodles
Stuffed Grape Leaves
Watercress and Basil Sauce
Broccoli and Ricotta Sauce
Greek Tomato Sauce
Pumpkin Seed Pesto
Mushroom and Pistachio Sauce
Creamy Sweet Pepper Sauce

Sweets and Treats
Fruit Salad From Kariba
Creamy Grape Dressing for Fruit Salads
Blueberry-Orange *Coulis*
Strawberry-Pear Puree
Pear Fans in Mango Puree
Pears and Plantains
Glazed Fresh Peaches with Apricot Preserve
Orange-Almond Custard
African Corn and Peanut Pudding
Dried Fruit Compote
Dessert Crepes
Warm Citrus Compote
Crunchy Candied Nuts
In Banana Heaven
Peach Filling for a Tart or Pie
Raisin-Oat Granola
Cool Raspberry and Rhubarb Sauce

20 Minutes or Under

The Healthier Happy Hour
Eggplant with Earthy Flavors
Irish Nachos
Fragrant Mussels
Clams with Spring Vegetable Puree
Scallops with Green Curry Sauce

Sensational Soups
Creamy Zucchini Soup with Lump Crab Garnish
Spicy Squash Soup with Matching Croutons
Shrimp and Smoked Salmon Bisque
Thai Lemongrass Soup with Shrimp and Scallions

From the Garden
Stuffed Whole Onions
Puree of Winter Squash with Rosemary

Braised Leeks with Warm Tomato Vinaigrette
Japanese Eggplant Salad
Warm Zucchini Mousse with Tomato Sauce and
  Mozzarella

From Rivers and Seas
Red Snapper with Jalapeño Butter
Mussels with Tomatoes and Fresh Basil
Clams with Cucumber-Leek Sauce
Seafood Sausage with Avocado Cream
Louisiana Catfish with Ya-Ya Rice
Frog Leg Salad with White Beans and Tiny Pasta

Birds of a Feather
Chicken Scallopini with Tomato Butter and Ziti
Happy Family Pancake
Chicken with Starfruit and Chilies
Chicken with Coconut Curry *(Adobo)*
Mustard-Poached Chicken with Zucchini Relish
Honey Chicken on Rice

New Wave Meats
Venison Sauce
Greek Meatballs *(Keftedes)*
Tornedos of Beef with Garlic-Jalapeño Puree
Soft Tortillas with *Piccadillo* Filling

Enlightened Entrées
Enchiladas with Sweet and Hot Chilies
Cabbage Bundles
Spaghetti Torte with Garlic and Peppers
Eggplant Steaks with Black Bean Sauce
Fresh Egg Rolls

Sweets and Treats
Rice Pudding with Cardamom and Almonds
Peach Bread Pudding with Pecans

THE HEALTHIER HAPPY HOUR

Scores of sources suggest that eating lighter, more nutritious foods may actually help us live longer. Microwaving, as you know, can help reduce fat, cholesterol, calories and sodium from our diets. And adding the right appetizers can support the cause.

Offer a light, microwaved appetizer as a first course. Eaten slowly it will help control your appetite. It's a relaxing and sociable way to begin a meal, in contrast to stressfully bolting down dinner.

When friends pop over for a visit, you can whip up a healthful microwaved snack in no time. Some of the recipes in this chapter, like Crisp Wonton Fans, take only about a minute.

You'll also find these minute-or-two recipes helpful when planning a large party. Stuffed mushroom caps, for instance, can be blanched in the microwave ahead of time and filled. When you're ready to serve, simply microwave on full power until the filling is heated through.

A sampling of two or three interesting appetizers can be a light and entertaining meal in itself. Try Wontons Filled with Rice and Chives, Snow Peas with Two Dipping Sauces and Scallops with Green Curry Sauce. It's an easy, low-fat, low salt menu that will serve four.

Turn on the Light

After trying the recipes in this book, I can almost guarantee you'll be coming up with lots of menu ideas on your own. Here are a few more to help get you started.

- Country Pâté, Marinated Chevre with Rosemary and Garlic and Cherry Tomato Cocktail served with crusty bread.
- Fish Pâté with Dill and Onions, artichokes with a dipping sauce and crusty bread
- Shrimp with Garlic-Almond Pesto, Favas, Italian Style and a salad of mixed lettuces

ESCARGOTS WITH SHALLOT BUTTER

4 servings • 77 calories per serving

2 tsp	sweet butter	10 ml
2	shallots, very finely minced	
	juice and pulp of 1 lemon	
2 tsp	very finely minced fresh parsley	10 ml
16	large escargots (1 can)	
	crusty bread for serving	

Combine the butter and shallots in a 9-inch (23-cm) glass pie dish and cover with vented plastic wrap. Microwave on full power until the shallots have just wilted, 1½ to 2 minutes.

To the same dish add the lemon, parsley and escargots. Scoot the escargots over to the edge of the dish, cover and microwave on full power until cooked through, about 1½ minutes. Let stand for another minute before serving with crusty bread to soak up the sauce.

Ideas for Serving Escargots

- In blanched mushroom caps sprinkled with freshly grated Parmesan
- In escargot shells
- Tossed with pasta

FAVAS, ITALIAN STYLE

Fresh fava beans come in big khaki pods, usually six beans to a pod. Split the pods open and you'll find big light green beans, each with a little brown smile.

If you can't find fresh favas, substitute 12 ounces (340 g) of rinsed, canned favas and shorten the cooking time to 3 to 3½ minutes.

4 servings • 166 calories per serving

2 lb	favas (in their pods)	1 kg
⅔ cup	beef stock	160 ml
3	cloves garlic, very finely minced	
1 Tbs	red wine vinegar	15 ml
1 tsp	oregano	5 ml
1	bay leaf	
1	small onion, sliced and separated into rings	
2 tsp	olive oil	10 ml
1 tsp	freshly squeezed lemon juice	5 ml
	freshly ground black pepper to taste	
	freshly grated Parmesan to taste	
	crusty Italian bread for serving	

Remove the favas from their pods and rinse. Then dump them into a 9-inch (23-cm) glass pie dish and add in the stock, garlic, vinegar, oregano, bay leaf and onion rings. Cover with vented plastic wrap and microwave on full power until tender, 8½ to 9 minutes, stirring midway.

Immediately stir in the olive oil, lemon juice, pepper and Parmesan and let stand for 5 minutes.

Serve scooped on crusty Italian bread after removing bay leaf.

Note: The favas make a nice light entrée tossed with pasta and chopped ripe tomatoes.

SNOW PEAS
WITH TWO
DIPPING SAUCES

The low-fat sauces can be served at room temperature or warmed, with other vegetables.

To ensure even cooking, choose snow peas that are all about the same size. Three to 4 inches is best. If you have smaller ones, the cooking time will be shorter.

4 servings • 7 calories per serving

1 lb	snow peas	450 g
Sauce from Singapore		
¼ cup	chicken stock	60 ml
1 tsp	mushroom soy sauce* or light soy sauce	5 ml
splash	toasted sesame oil	
All-American Sauce		
¼ cup	fresh spinach leaves	60 ml
1	scallion, coarsely chopped	
¼ cup	buttermilk	60 ml
pinch	freshly ground allspice	

To prepare the peas, pinch off the little stem tops with your fingernails and zip the strings clear down the sides. This won't take as long as it sounds, especially if you get a rhythm going or do it to music.

Rinse the peas, then dump them, still wet, into a 9-inch (23-cm) glass pie dish. Cover with vented plastic wrap and microwave on full power until just tender, 2½ to 3½ minutes. Let stand 1 minute.

Meanwhile, prepare the sauces. For the one from Singapore, combine the stock, soy sauce and sesame oil in a small dish. Cover with vented plastic wrap and microwave on full power until warm, 15 to 20 seconds.

For the American sauce, combine the spinach, scallions, buttermilk and allspice in a processor and whiz until smooth. Scoop into a small dish, cover with vented plastic wrap and microwave on full power until warm, about 15 seconds.

To serve, arrange the peas on a pretty serving dish around little cups of sauces.

*Available at Oriental markets.

MUSHROOM CAPS WITH PECANS AND BASIL

You can prevent tearing mushroom caps if you insert the tip of a teaspoon around the base of the stem before removing.

4 servings • 90 calories per serving

12	large mushrooms, stems removed	
2 Tbs	coarsely chopped fresh basil leaves	30 ml
3 Tbs	chopped pecans	45 ml
1 tsp	sweet butter	5 ml
	olive oil for painting, if necessary	
	freshly grated Parmesan for sprinkling	

Rinse the mushroom caps and arrange them, still wet, around the edge of a 9-inch (23-cm) glass pie dish. Cover with vented plastic wrap and microwave on full power until they appear blanched, about 1 minute. Gently scoop them into a strainer and let them drain while you prepare the filling.

Preheat a browning dish according to manufacturer's instructions, which will probably be about 4 minutes.

Combine the basil, pecans and butter in a processor and whiz just until you have tiny crumbs. Use a baby spoon to stuff the mixture into the mushroom caps and have them ready, near the microwave.

If the browning dish has a surface that may stick, paint it with a bit of oil after preheating. Then quickly set the caps on the dish, filling side up, and microwave, uncovered, for about 2½ minutes. Imme-diately sprinkle on the Parmesan and let stand 3 minutes. Serve warm.

More Ideas for Fillings

After you've completed the blanching step you can fill the caps with whatever you like. Here are some tasty suggestions:

- Minced cooked mussels and minced leeks with a splash of light cream
- Minced cooked eggplant with a garlicky tomato sauce
- Minced crabmeat, minced fresh dill and a splash of light cream
- Corn bread stuffing and pecans
- White bean puree with minced fresh parsley and garlic

Modern Artichokes

Forget the special steamers and baskets. They're old-fashioned. The new trend in preparing artichokes is right in your microwave.

It's best to microwave two artichokes at a time. Use a knife to trim the stem ends so they'll stand up straight for serving. Then use scissors to snip off the leaf tips.

Wrap each artichoke in a damp paper towel and microwave on full power until a leaf pulls away easily, about 7 minutes, turning and rotating midway.

Let the artichokes stand until cool enough to handle, about 5 to 6 minutes.

Dipping Sauces for Artichokes

Peel off a leaf and dip it into a flavorful sauce. When you reach the bottom, cut it into chunks and let marinate for a few minutes in the sauce.

- Combine equal parts of blue cheese and skim milk, cover with vented plastic wrap and microwave on medium power until the cheese has softened.
- Warm herbed vinaigrette about 15 seconds in the microwave.
- Puree an avocado, then mix with freshly squeezed lemon juice and a pinch of dry mustard.
- Crumble a pinch of saffron threads and microwave in orange juice until fragrant. Then stir into thick, plain, low-fat yogurt.

How to Stuff Artichokes

Gently spread the leaves (of a microwaved artichoke) apart and use a grapefruit spoon to remove the hairy choke. Then fill with:

- Minced cooked bay scallops and minced roasted sweet peppers
- Salmon mousse
- Pasta salad
- Chopped spinach with fresh basil and mozzarella cheese, microwaved on medium power until the mozzarella has melted
- Eggplant Dunk with Garlic Studs (page 40)

You can also scoop the pulp from the leaves with a grapefruit spoon, puree it and use in soups and sauces. You'll get about ¼ cup (60 ml) from one artichoke. And don't forget to enjoy the tender bottoms, marinated or pureed for soups and sauces.

RAGOUT
OF WILD MUSHROOMS

Don't let the "wild" scare you. If you can't find the recommended ones, use what's available in your area. Cultivated and field mushrooms will work just fine.

4 servings • 81 calories per serving

Preheat a browning dish according to manufacturer's instructions, which will probably be about 4 minutes.

Meanwhile, in a large bowl, combine the mushrooms, ginger, garlic, soy sauce, Worcestershire and peanut oil and toss.

If the browning dish has a surface that may stick, paint a bit of oil on it after it's been preheated. Then quickly set each mushroom, stem side down, on the browning dish and cover very loosely with waxed paper. This is to prevent splattering.

10	fresh crimini mushrooms	
10	fresh shiitake mushrooms, stems removed	
10	oyster mushrooms	
½ tsp	very finely minced fresh ginger	2 ml
1	clove garlic, very finely minced	
½ tsp	mushroom soy sauce* or light soy sauce	2 ml
1 tsp	Worcestershire sauce	5 ml
1 tsp	peanut oil	5 ml
	peanut oil for painting, if necessary	
½ cup	watercress leaves	120 ml

Microwave on full power for about 1 minute and 20 seconds, then let stand for 1 minute. Toss with the watercress and serve hot in ramekins or little dishes.

*Available at Oriental markets.

EGGPLANT
WITH EARTHY FLAVORS

Use dried tomatoes that have been packed without salt.

4 servings • 108 calories per serving

1		eggplant (1 lb or 450 g), cut into chunks	
5		dried tomatoes, minced	
5		dried porcini mushrooms, minced	
3		bay leaves	
2	Tbs	beef stock	30 ml
2	tsp	olive oil	10 ml
3		roasted peppers, sliced	
		freshly ground black pepper to taste	
		freshly grated Romano cheese to taste	
		curly endive for serving	

Combine the eggplant, tomatoes, mushrooms, bay leaves, beef stock and olive oil in a 9-inch (23-cm) glass pie dish and cover with vented plastic wrap. Microwave on full power until the eggplant chunks have softened and almost collapsed, about 7 minutes, stirring midway. Let stand 5 minutes, then remove bay leaves.

Stir in the roasted peppers, black pepper and Romano and combine well. Serve warm on beds of curly endive.

CHERRY TOMATO COCKTAIL

4 servings • 41 calories per serving

1 lb	firm cherry tomatoes	450 g
2	scallions, very finely minced	
2 Tbs	very finely minced fresh mint	30 ml
1 Tbs	champagne vinegar or white wine vinegar	15 ml
1½ tsp	hazelnut oil	7 ml
1 cup	finely shredded watercress or spinach	240 ml

Rinse the tomatoes and scoop them, still wet, into a 9-inch (23-cm) glass pie dish. Cover with vented plastic wrap and microwave on full power for about 2 minutes. Some tomatoes may pop and that's OK.

Immediately dump the tomatoes into ice water, then into a strainer to drain.

When they're cool enough to handle, peel. This may sound too fussy, but with a sharp paring knife and some determination, each tomato only takes about 30 seconds.

In a medium bowl combine the scallions, mint, vinegar and oil and add in the tomatoes. Let marinate for 1 hour at room temperature.

To serve, fill 4 glasses or wine goblets with the watercress or spinach, then scoop in the tomatoes and serve at room temperature with long teaspoons.

IRISH NACHOS

Potatoes are used instead of the traditional fried corn chips.

4 servings • 155 calories per serving

¾ lb	waxy-type potatoes, thinly sliced	340 g
2	tomatoes, chopped	
2	scallions, minced	
1	large, mild, green chili pepper, chopped	
1	jalapeño pepper, seeded and minced (wear plastic gloves when handling)	
½ tsp	chili powder	2 ml
½ tsp	oregano	2 ml
⅔ cup	grated mild white cheese	160 ml

Arrange the potatoes in a 9-inch (23-cm) glass pie dish and sprinkle with a splash of water. Cover with vented plastic wrap and microwave on full power until tender, 5 to 6 minutes, rotating the dish midway. Let stand 4 minutes.

If necessary, drain the potatoes. Sprinkle the tomatoes on top of them. Next, sprinkle on the scallions, chilies, jalapeños, chili powder, oregano and cheese and cover with vented plastic wrap. Microwave on medium power until the cheese has melted, about 3 minutes. Then run it under the broiler until just brown. Serve hot.

In the Chips

Make your own tortilla chips without frying: Cut two flour tortillas into eighths. Then set them on a paper-towel-lined plate and microwave, uncovered, on full power until crisp, about 3½ minutes. Serve with dips, salsas and refried beans.

Or make nachos by sprinkling grated cheddar, minced jalapeños (wear plastic gloves when handling) and minced chives onto just-microwaved flour tortilla chips. Microwave, uncovered, on medium power until the cheese has melted.

Soft corn tortillas take about 3 minutes to turn into chips when microwaved in this manner. Use them as you would flour chips but don't make nachos because they can get soggy.

FISH PÂTÉ WITH DILL AND ONIONS

Spread on cucumber rounds or crusty bread with lemon wedges for squeezing. If you're in the mood to fuss a bit, the pâté makes a tasty filling for ravioli or tortellini.

Makes about 2 cups • 99 calories per ¼-cup serving

½ lb	bass, rockfish, grouper or other meaty pink fish	225 g
1 Tbs	lemon juice	15 ml
1	small onion, chopped	
1 tsp	sweet butter	5 ml
¼ lb	smoked salmon	115 g
1 tsp	dillweed	5 ml
1 tsp	Dijon-style mustard	5 ml
1 tsp	prepared horseradish	5 ml
3 Tbs	minced fresh chives	45 ml
1 cup	thick, plain, low-fat yogurt	240 ml

Combine the bass or other pink fish, lemon juice, onions and butter in a 9-inch (23-cm) glass pie dish and cover with vented plastic wrap. Microwave on full power until the fish is cooked through, about 3 minutes. Let stand for 3 minutes.

Drain the fish and dump it into a processor along with the salmon, dillweed, mustard, horseradish and chives. Process with 5 or 6 on/off pulses, leaving tiny chunks of fish. Don't make a puree.

Chill the pâté for at least 2 hours. Fold in the yogurt before serving.

CRISP WONTON FANS

*Here's a major culinary breakthrough—
crisp wontons that aren't deep-fried.*

Makes a dozen chips • 24 calories per chip

Arrange the wonton triangles (points toward center) on a paper-towel-lined plate. Brush with the butter, sprinkle with thyme and oregano and microwave, uncovered, on full power until crisp, about 1½ minutes.

Sprinkle with the Parmesan and microwave, uncovered, on medium power until

6	square wonton skins, cut diagonally into triangles	
2 tsp	sweet butter, melted	10 ml
pinch	thyme	
pinch	oregano	
	freshly grated Parmesan for sprinkling	

melted, about 20 seconds.

These are nice served warm or room temperature from a pretty basket lined with a crisp linen napkin.

Make Your Own Low-Fat Cream Cheese

This is so easy and delicious that you'll make it all the time. Its texture is between a cream and cottage cheese and the taste is mild. And unlike many cheeses of this type, it contains no added salt.

Makes about ⅓ cup • 42 calories per Tbs

1 cup	buttermilk	240 ml
1 cup	milk	240 ml

Combine the buttermilk and milk in a 2-quart (2-liter) dish. Cover and microwave on full power until the whey (thin pearly liquid) separates out, the curds form a solid mass in the middle and bubbles appear around the edge of the dish. This will take 4 to 4½ minutes. Don't boil hard or the curds will become rubbery. And don't stir.

Set the dish aside, covered with a paper towel until completely cool, about 3 hours. Don't cheat or your cheese will be too watery.

Drain the cheese through a paper-towel-lined strainer until all the whey is gone. Stir well, then store covered and refrigerated for about a week.

Useful Ideas

- Use as a filling for blintzes and crepes
- Mix with smoked bluefish and spread on cucumber rounds
- Serve atop fresh fruit for breakfast
- Spread on crusty bread and top with thinly sliced smoked salmon

WONTONS FILLED WITH RICE AND CHIVES

Makes 8 wontons • 38 calories per wonton

¼ cup	cooked rice	60 ml
2 Tbs	minced fresh chives	30 ml
¾ tsp	light soy sauce	3 ml
¼ tsp	very finely minced fresh ginger	1 ml
1	clove garlic, very finely minced	
8	square or round wonton skins	
1 Tbs	sweet butter	15 ml

Combine the rice, chives, soy sauce, ginger and garlic in a small bowl and keep it handy.

Lightly paint the perimeter of a wonton skin with butter and spoon a bit of filling on one half. Press the wonton tightly shut and repeat with remaining wontons and filling.

Arrange the wontons around the rim of a paper-towel-lined plate and paint them with the remaining butter. Microwave, uncovered, on full power until crisp, 2 to 3 minutes. Watch them so they don't burn and let stand for 2 minutes before serving.

More Ideas for Fillings

- Minced broccoli and minced scallion
- Tiny shrimp with garlic and ginger
- Minced fresh crab with a bit of herb butter
- Minced cooked beef with garlic, hot pepper sauce and a grated orange peel

It's tempting to imagine filling the wontons with cheese, but it becomes too rubbery when cooked on full power, and the wontons become too gummy when cooked on medium power.

If you're really in the mood for cheese, sprinkle it on the wontons just as they're taken from the microwave. The cheese, if finely grated, will melt during standing time.

MARINATED CHEVRE WITH ROSEMARY AND GARLIC

If you can't find chevre, use any soft, white creamy cheese.

4 servings • 175 calories per serving

¼ cup	cider vinegar		60 ml
1 Tbs	olive oil		15 ml
1 Tbs	minced fresh rosemary leaves		15 ml
¼ tsp	Dijon-style mustard		1 ml
1	clove garlic, very finely minced		
½ lb	chevre or soft, white creamy cheese		225 g
½ cup	dry bread crumbs		120 ml
	coarse bread for serving		
	endive petals for serving		

Combine the vinegar, oil, rosemary, mustard and garlic in a 9-inch (23-cm) glass pie dish. Cover with vented plastic wrap and microwave on full power until fragrant but not boiling, about 1 minute.

Meanwhile, form the chevre or other soft cheese into "golf balls" and press them into disks. Press the disks lightly into the bread crumbs, then set them in the marinade. Refrigerate for 30 minutes, flipping the disks midway.

When you're ready to serve, cover the dish with vented plastic wrap and microwave on medium power until the cheese is soft and warm but not melting, about 1 minute.

Serve with coarse bread and endive petals.

Quick Tomato and Feta Sandwich

Set a ripe tomato slice on a paper-towel-lined saucer. Sprinkle it with crumbled feta cheese and sprinkle the feta with a bit of oregano. Cover with a matching tomato slice. Then cover with plastic wrap and microwave on medium power for about 1 minute. Let stand for 1 minute before serving on a bed of crisp greens.

SHRIMP WITH GARLIC-ALMOND PESTO

Great light dinner or brunch fare.

4 servings • 177 calories per serving

Combine the garlic, Parmesan, oregano or mint, parsley, almonds, vinegar and oil in a spice grinder or processor and whiz until you have a smooth paste.

In a medium bowl, toss the shrimp with the paste until well coated. Then arrange them around the edge of a large, round plate. Cover with vented plastic wrap and microwave on full power until the shrimp are cooked through, about 4 minutes. Let stand for 2 minutes, then cover and refrigerate.

3	cloves garlic, coarsely chopped	
1 Tbs	freshly grated Parmesan	15 ml
1 Tbs	minced fresh oregano or mint	15 ml
1 Tbs	minced fresh parsley	15 ml
20	almonds	
2 Tbs	red wine vinegar	30 ml
1 Tbs	olive oil	15 ml
1 lb	large shrimp, shelled and deveined	450 g
	red lettuce leaves for serving	
	lemon wedges for drizzling	

Serve chilled with red lettuce leaves and lemon wedges for drizzling.

FRAGRANT MUSSELS

This is a nice recipe in which to use New Zealand Mussels, or Kiwi Clams (if you can get them in your area; if not, the local product will do just fine). These are larger than the blue mussels we know in the U.S. and the flesh of the male is ivory while the female is pink. The male and female taste the same but the female has a softer texture. They're available fresh or frozen on the half shell and the fresh can be microwaved for about 2 minutes per dozen on full power. The frozen (don't defrost) require 4 minutes per dozen on full power.

4 servings • 54 calories per serving

1 Tbs	rice vinegar	15 ml
	juice and pulp of 1 lime	
1 Tbs	minced fresh basil	15 ml
1 Tbs	minced fresh mint	15 ml
¼ tsp	hot pepper sauce, or to taste	1 ml
2	cloves garlic, very finely minced	
24	mussels	

In a 9-inch (23-cm) glass pie dish combine the vinegar, lime, basil, mint, hot pepper sauce and garlic. Add half of the mussels, cover with vented plastic wrap and microwave on full power until they have opened, up to 4 minutes. Remove mussels and cover with foil to keep them warm. Repeat with the remaining half of the mussels.

To serve, arrange mussels in individual shallow bowls and pour the sauce over them.

Hot Stuff

Create an easy hot beverage for a cold winter's night by combining equal parts of tomato juice and beef stock. Add a dash of Worcestershire or hot pepper sauce and microwave on full power until warm. One cup will take about 1 to 1½ minutes.

EGGPLANT DUNK
WITH GARLIC STUDS

Serve with an array of raw vegetables or with crusty bread.

Makes about ⅔ cup • 48 calories per Tbs

1	eggplant (½ lb or 225 g)	
4	cloves garlic	
	olive oil for rubbing	
½ tsp	oregano	2 ml
3 Tbs	tahini (sesame paste)	45 ml
2 Tbs	coarsely chopped fresh parsley	30 ml
¼ cup	milk	60 ml
¼ tsp	curry powder	1 ml

Peel the eggplant and cut it vertically into quarters. Then use the tip of your knife to make 8 little slits in each quarter. The slits are for the garlic studs.

To prepare the garlic, slice each clove into 8 studs. Put a garlic stud in each slit.

Rub the eggplant quarters on all sides with olive oil and set them into a large, flat dish that's big enough for them to lie unstacked. Sprinkle on the oregano, cover with vented plastic wrap and microwave on full power until tender, 5 to 6 minutes. Let stand for 5 minutes.

Cut the eggplant quarters into manageable chunks and toss them into a processor along with the tahini, parsley, milk and curry powder. Whip until you have a smooth paste. Serve warm or chilled.

CLAMS WITH SPRING VEGETABLE PUREE

If clams aren't your pleasure, try the puree with crab legs or shrimp.

4 servings • 57 calories per serving

⅓ cup	watercress leaves	80 ml
¼ cup	coarsely chopped fresh parsley	60 ml
1 cup	fresh spinach	240 ml
2	scallions, chopped	
3	sprigs fresh thyme or ½ tsp (2 ml) dried	
2 Tbs	ricotta cheese	30 ml
2 Tbs	milk	30 ml
1 Tbs	freshly grated Parmesan	15 ml
16	littleneck clams, rinsed and scrubbed	
	watercress sprigs for garnishing	

In a 9-inch (23-cm) glass pie dish combine the watercress, parsley, spinach, scallions and thyme. Cover with vented plastic wrap and microwave on full power until the greens have wilted and reduced in volume, 3½ to 4 minutes. Let stand for 2 minutes.

Scoop the greens into a processor or blender and whiz until pureed. With the motor running, add in the ricotta, milk and Parmesan and whiz until smooth. Let the sauce sit while you prepare the clams.

Set as many clams as will fit along the rim of a large, round plate with the part that opens facing the center. Cover with a damp paper towel and microwave on full power until the clams open, which should begin at about 2½ minutes. You may quickly remove the clams as they open to avoid overcooking. Discard clams that haven't opened in 5½ minutes. Repeat with remaining clams if necessary.

To serve, arrange the clams in their shells on individual serving dishes and top each with a spoonful of puree. Watercress sprigs make a nice garnish.

Notes:

- You'll have some puree left over. Jar and refrigerate it and serve with diced cooked potatoes for an interesting salad.
- If you really feel ambitious, remove the clams from their shells and chop. Toss with hot pasta and enough puree to sauce everything.

SCALLOPS WITH GREEN CURRY SAUCE

Serve with aromatic rice, like basmati, in shallow dishes or shells.

4 servings • 191 calories per serving

In a 9-inch (23-cm) glass pie dish combine the garlic, lemon juice, ginger, hot pepper sauce, stock, *nam pla* or soy sauce and butter. Cover with vented plastic wrap and microwave on full power for about 2 minutes.

Toss the scallops in the peanut oil and add them to the dish. Push them toward the edges, leaving a hole in the middle. Cover and microwave on full power until the scallops are cooked through, about 2½ minutes.

Immediately add the coriander, basil and coconut milk or milk and let stand, covered, for 3 minutes before serving hot.

3	cloves garlic, sliced	
1 Tbs	freshly squeezed lemon juice	15 ml
½ tsp	finely minced fresh ginger	2 ml
1 tsp	hot pepper sauce, or to taste	5 ml
3 Tbs	chicken stock	45 ml
1 Tbs	*nam pla** or light soy sauce	15 ml
1 Tbs	sweet butter	15 ml
1 lb	sea scallops	450 g
1 tsp	peanut oil	5 ml
1 Tbs	finely minced fresh coriander	15 ml
1 Tbs	finely minced fresh basil	15 ml
2 Tbs	Unsweetened Coconut Milk (page 151)† or milk	30 ml

*Nam pla is a dark, flavorful and pungent, fish-based sauce that's available at Oriental markets and specialty foods stores.
†Unsweetened coconut milk is also available at East Indian markets.

COUNTRY PÂTÉ

Here's a completely no-fat-added, no-salt-added pâté. Serve with coarse bread and condiments like mustard and cranberry sauce.

Makes 1 round pâté (8 servings) • 103 calories per serving

1 lb	chicken cutlets, chopped	450 g
½ lb	lean beef, chopped	225 g
1	shallot, chopped	
1	clove garlic, chopped	
1 tsp	sage	5 ml
½ tsp	thyme	2 ml
½ tsp	Dijon-style mustard	2 ml
3	bay leaves	

Combine the chicken, beef, shallots, garlic, sage, thyme and mustard in a processor and whiz with on/off pulses until finely chopped but not pureed.

Arrange the bay leaves in the bottom of a 7-inch (18-cm) microwave-safe ring pan (or loaf pan, if you wish) and scoop in the pâté. Press it in firmly, then cover with vented plastic wrap. Microwave on full power until cooked through, 7 to 8 minutes, rotating the dish midway.

If there's fat in the dish, carefully drain it. Then chill the pâté, covered, for at least 2 hours. Unmold chilled pâté onto a serving plate. To serve, cut into thin slices.

Give New Life to a Lemon

Have you ever discovered half a lemon in your refrigerator that appears to have lost all life? Place it face down on a damp paper towel and microwave on full power for about 20 seconds. Then juice or slice. This trick works with limes, too.

SENSATIONAL SOUPS

Soups are a great way to help keep your shape, or even lose some weight if that's what you have in mind. Studies from the University of Pennsylvania, University of Nebraska and the Swanson Center for Nutrition revealed that subjects who ate soup, especially hot soup, consumed fewer calories at a meal than subjects who didn't. One reason is that soup is made up of so much liquid, which can aid slimming because it acts to satisfy hunger pangs early in the meal. What's more, if soup is hot you'll tend to eat slowly so you'll know sooner when you're full.

Making your own soups gives you the opportunity to control salt and fat. And microwaving lets you shorten cooking time dramatically and retain nutrients. Besides, if you can create a homemade soup in a fraction of the original time, you'll be more encouraged to do it, especially on busy weeknights.

Generally, when microwaving soups, try to microwave the solids with a small amount of liquid, then add hot liquid later. This way soups will microwave faster and have bolder flavors. One obvious exception to this rule is when you're making stocks and other soups that must be microwaved with a large volume of liquid. In this case, be sure to use a cooking dish that's twice the volume of what you're microwaving, to avoid boilovers. Oiling the sides of the dish will help avoid boilovers, too.

Here are some other useful secrets concerning soup and the microwave.

- Clay cookware, the kind you soak in water before using, is a nice vessel in which to microwave and serve soups.
- When uncovering hot soups, use the cover to shield your face from the hot steam. If you're using plastic wrap, stand back as you remove it.
- Soup will defrost faster if it's been frozen in single-portion sizes in shallow containers.
- Don't reheat soups that contain milk in the microwave because they can become too frothy.
- Soups microwaved at high altitudes may need an extra minute or two of cooking time. This is especially true with stocks and other soups that must be microwaved with a large volume of liquid.

CHICKEN STOCK

Smacking the chicken bones, as done in this recipe, is an old Cajun trick to obtain a more flavorful stock.

Makes about a quart

Remove the skin from the chicken and smack the bones with the back of a heavy cleaver or mallet to break them up a bit. Toss them into a large, casserole-type dish and add the rest of the ingredients. Cover tightly and microwave on full power for about 20 minutes, stirring or shaking midway. Let stand for 20 minutes, then strain.

Refrigerate overnight. The fat will harden so that it can be lifted off easily. The stock freezes well.

¾ lb	chicken necks and backs	340 g
3	stalks celery, leaves too, chopped	
3	carrots, chopped	
handful	fresh parsley	
1	onion, skin too, quartered	
2	shallots, skin too, quartered	
1	dried mushroom, like porcini, chopped	
½ cup	dry white wine or nonalcoholic wine	120 ml
7	black peppercorns	
3½ cups	water, or to cover	840 ml

Variations:

- Instead of parsley, use fresh tarragon, rosemary or sage
- Add 3 slices of fresh ginger
- Add 3 fresh hot chili peppers
- Use leek instead of onion
- Add a pinch of saffron

BEEF STOCK

The bones and onions must be broiled to give the stock its rich flavor and color, which is especially important because of the absence of salt.

Makes about a quart

Preheat the broiler and arrange the bones on a broiler tray. Set the onions on the tray, skin side down, and broil until the bones are brown and fragrant, about 8 minutes on each side. Tip the bones and onions into a large, casserole-type dish and add the remaining ingredients. Cover and microwave on full power for about 20 minutes, then let stand for 20 minutes. Strain and refrigerate overnight. The fat will harden so that it can be lifted off easily. The stock freezes well.

1 lb	beef neck bones	450 g
1	yellow onion, skin too, quartered	
1	carrot, sliced	
1	turnip, sliced	
handful	fresh parsley	
1	stalk celery, leaves too, chopped	
1 tsp	coriander seeds	5 ml
1 tsp	black peppercorns	5 ml
¼ cup	dry red wine or nonalcoholic wine	60 ml
4 cups	water, or to cover	1 liter

Quick Soups from Beef Stock

- Combine half tomato juice and half Beef Stock. Serve hot, garnished with minced fresh chives.
- Pour hot Beef Stock into bowls containing cooked rice or tiny pasta.

GARDEN STOCK

The onions are broiled to give the stock color and rich flavor in the absence of salt.

Makes about a quart

Preheat the broiler. Toss the onion slices in a bit of olive oil and arrange them on a broiler tray. Broil until toasty brown, 4 to 5 minutes on each side.

Tip the onions into a large, casserole-type dish and add the remaining ingredients. Cover and microwave on full power for about 20 minutes. Let stand for 20 minutes, strain and use. The stock freezes well.

Quick Soups from Garden Stock

- Slice bay scallops into thin coins and toss them into individual serving bowls. Then pour in hot Garden Stock and the scallop coins will

2	onions, skin too, sliced into 6 pieces	
	olive oil for tossing	
2	carrots, sliced	
1	turnip, sliced	
1 cup	chopped winter squash	240 ml
1½ cups	broccoli rabe or spinach	360 ml
¼ cup	fresh dark mushrooms, like crimini, chopped	60 ml
1	stalk celery, chopped	
1	bay leaf	
pinch	tarragon	
3½ cups	water, or to cover	840 ml

cook in an instant. Garnish with finely minced scallions.
- Add shredded cooked chicken and a bit of minced fresh ginger to hot Garden Stock. Garnish with toasted sesame seeds.
- Add cooked thin noodles and baby peas to hot Garden Stock. Garnish with minced fresh mint.

UNCLASSIC FUMET

Here's a fish stock with its origins in 17th century France. Its preparation has clearly taken on some space-age characteristics.

Makes about a quart

Combine all of the ingredients in a large, casserole-type dish and cover. Microwave on full power for about 15 minutes, then let stand for 15 minutes. Strain before using. The *fumet* freezes well.

Useful Ideas

- Serve hot with a confetti of vegetables and flaked crab

	shells from 1 lb of shrimp, rinsed	
3 cups	water	720 ml
½ cup	dry white wine or nonalcoholic wine	120 ml
¼	lemon, skin too, chopped	
1	carrot, chopped	
1	onion, skin too, quartered	
1	stalk celery, chopped	
3	bay leaves	
5	black peppercorns	
1	sprig fresh parsley	

- Use as a base for clam chowders
- Use as a base for *cioppino* or *bouillabaisse*
- Use as a base for fish sauces

Quick Garnishes for Soups

- Julienne of kale, chard or spinach
- Ribbons of citrus peel
- Cooked omelette strips
- Minced chives
- Chopped cooked shrimp
- Dill, parsley or other fresh herb sprigs
- Minced cooked egg white
- Toasted sesame seeds
- Cinnamon stick for fruit soups

JAPANESE FISH STOCK (DASHI)

This stock is one of the foundations of Japanese cooking. It's used as a flavoring, in sauces and, of course, as a soup base. It's a light golden color and tastes smoky sweet. Its characteristic taste comes from **bonito,** *which is shaved, dried fish with a rich smoky flavor.* **Bonito** *is a good salt alternative.*

Makes about a quart

Combine all of the ingredients in a large, casserole-type dish and cover. Microwave on full power for about 4 minutes. Let stand for 5 minutes. Strain and use hot.

4 cups	water	1 liter
1	piece of *kombu**	
1 cup	*bonito**	240 ml
¼ cup	*mirin**	60 ml

Useful Ideas

- Use instead of water for simmering vegetables
- Serve as a light soup with shredded spinach and minced cooked salmon
- Serve as a light soup with snow peas and shrimp
- Serve as a light soup with shredded smoked turkey and minced scallions

*Available at Oriental markets.

CLEAR BROTH WITH SEE-THROUGH WONTONS

The beautiful color and pattern of the cilantro is visible through the wonton skins.

4 servings • 62 calories per serving

1	slice fresh ginger	
1 tsp	peanut oil	5 ml
4 cups	chicken stock or	1 liter
	Japanese Fish Stock	
	(Dashi), page 50	
8	thin wonton skins	
8	sprigs fresh cilantro	
	minced scallions for	
	garnishing	
	sesame oil for garnishing	
	toasted sesame seeds for	
	garnishing	

Combine the ginger, oil and stock in a large, casserole-type dish, cover and microwave on full power until hot, about 5 minutes.

Meanwhile, lay the wontons out on a dry counter and set a sprig of cilantro on one half of each. Use a finger to rub the perimeter of each wonton with water, then fold in half and press closed. Spread the wontons on a paper towel and microwave on full power for 1 minute. Divide the wontons among 4 bowls.

Pour the hot stock over the wontons and let stand for a couple of minutes before serving with garnishes.

EGG FLOWER SOUP

4 servings • 37 calories per serving

4 cups	chicken stock or	1 liter
	Japanese Fish Stock	
	(Dashi), page 50	
1	egg, beaten	
¼ cup	minced fresh chives	60 ml
splash	chili oil	

Pour the stock into a large, casserole-type dish, cover and microwave until hot but not boiling, about 5 minutes. Remove the dish from the microwave, give the egg a stir and pour it into the hot stock. Immediately stir once to break up the egg and suddenly, delicate flower petals will appear. Serve hot sprinkled with minced chives and chili oil.

Variations:

- Add chopped cooked shrimp or shredded cooked chicken to the individual serving bowls before pouring the soup in.
- Add sliced baby corn or corn kernels to the individual bowls before pouring the soup in.

Hot Bowls and Mugs

Heated bowls or mugs are a nice touch for serving hot soups. First rinse two to four bowls or mugs in water, shake them off, then set them in the microwave. Cover with a sheet of plastic wrap and microwave on full power until hot, about 2 minutes.

Ragout of Wild Mushrooms (page 30)

Cherry Tomato Cocktail (page 32)

Irish Nachos (page 33)

Country Pâté (page 43)

Clear Broth with See-Through Wontons (page 51)

Shrimp and Smoked Salmon Bisque (page 67)

Lemon Miso Soup with Vegetable Julienne and Skinny Noodles (page 75)

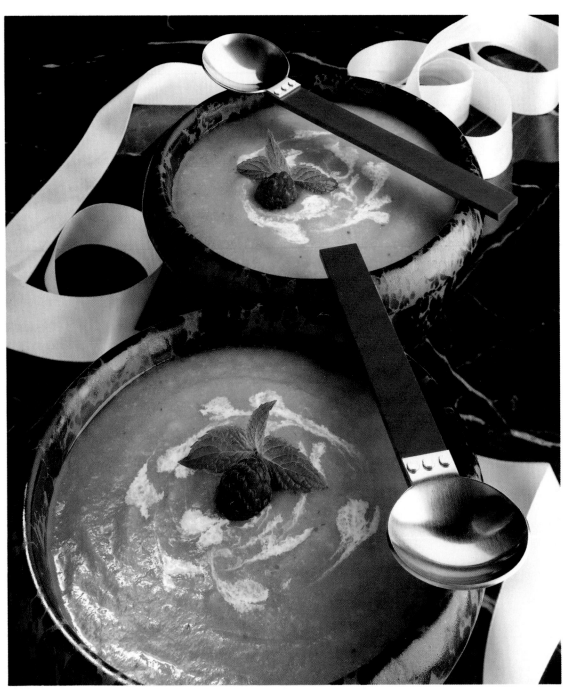

Creamy Peach Soup (page 77)

CREAMY ZUCCHINI SOUP WITH LUMP CRAB GARNISH

4 servings • 93 calories per serving

Combine the zucchini, onions, dillweed, bay leaves, chili powder and lemon juice in a 9-inch (23-cm) glass pie dish, cover with vented plastic wrap and microwave on full power until the vegetables are tender, about 6 minutes. Stir or shake midway. Let stand while you prepare the rest of the soup.

Wrap the crab in waxed paper and microwave on full power until pink and firm, about 30 seconds, then set it aside.

Microwave the stock on full power, covered, in a convenient container until heated through, about 1 minute.

Now you're ready to assemble the soup. Remove the bay leaves from the zucchini mixture and pour half of it into a processor or blender and puree, then

1 lb	zucchini, grated	450 g
1	onion, chopped	
½ tsp	dillweed	2 ml
2	bay leaves	
pinch	hot, Mexican-type chili powder	
1 tsp	lemon juice	5 ml
3 oz.	lump crab	85 g
1 cup	chicken stock	240 ml
1 cup	milk, warmed in microwave	240 ml

scoop it into a large bowl. Add the other half of the zucchini, the stock and the milk and stir to combine. Pour the soup into individual bowls, garnish with the crab and serve.

To serve chilled, do not heat the stock; simply refrigerate before serving.

SPICY SQUASH SOUP WITH MATCHING CROUTONS

4 servings • 246 calories per serving

1	onion, chopped	
10 oz	chopped squash or pumpkin	280 g
2	scallions, minced	
2 Tbs	chopped celery leaves	30 ml
¼ cup	chicken stock	60 ml
¼ cup	peanut butter	60 ml
10	drops hot pepper sauce	
1½ cups	milk, warmed in microwave	360 ml
1½ tsp	sweet butter	7 ml
¼ tsp	oregano	1 ml
¼ tsp	hot, Mexican-type chili powder	1 ml
pinch	ground allspice	
2	slices bread, cubed	

Combine the onions, squash or pumpkin, scallions, celery and stock in a 9-inch (23-cm) glass pie dish, cover with vented plastic wrap and microwave on full power until the vegetables are tender, about 5½ minutes. Stir or shake midway.

Scoop the mixture into a processor or blender. Add the peanut butter, hot pepper sauce and milk and whiz until smooth and combined. Let the soup relax while you make the croutons.

In a small dish combine the butter, oregano, chili powder and allspice. Cover with vented plastic wrap and microwave on full power until the butter is melted, about 40 seconds. Toss with the bread cubes until they're coated, then spread the cubes out onto a sheet of waxed paper and microwave until they're the texture of croutons, about 2½ minutes. Serve the soup room temperature or warm, sprinkled with the croutons.

SWEET POTATO VICHYSSOISE

This soup breaks two traditional rules. First, it uses sweet potatoes rather than white ones, and second, it's served warm instead of chilled.

4 servings • 159 calories per serving

Combine the sweet potatoes, leeks, onions and shallots in a 9-inch (23-cm) glass pie dish, cover with vented plastic wrap and microwave on full power until the vegetables are tender, about 6 minutes. Stir or shake midway.

Scoop the vegetables into a processor or blender and whiz until smooth. Process or stir in the mustard, nutmeg, light cream or milk and stock and serve warm.

¾ lb	sweet potatoes, peeled and cut into chunks	340 g
2	leeks, cleaned and chopped	
1	onion, chopped	
1	shallot, chopped	
1 tsp	Dijon-style mustard	5 ml
pinch	freshly grated nutmeg	
⅓ cup	light cream or milk, warmed in microwave	80 ml
1 cup	chicken stock, room temperature	240 m

Corn Ribbons

Here's a quick, crisp garnish for soups. Corn ribbons are especially nice with tomato and other vegetable soups. Start with a fresh corn tortilla and slice it into very thin ribbons. Lay them out on a paper towel in a single layer and microwave, uncovered, on full power until crisp, about 2 minutes. Then sprinkle over hot soup.

TOMATO SOUP WITH TUNA AND FRESH BASIL

4 servings • 75 calories per serving

2 tsp	sweet butter, softened	10 ml
1 tsp	curry powder	5 ml
¼ cup	minced fresh basil	60 ml
2 cups	tomatoes, peeled, seeded and crushed	480 ml
1½ cups	tomato juice	360 ml
½ cup	water-packed tuna, drained	120 ml
	minced black olives for garnishing	

Set the butter in a 9-inch (23-cm) glass pie dish and cover with vented plastic wrap. Microwave on full power until the butter has melted, about 30 seconds. Stir in curry powder and basil and microwave on full power for 20 seconds. Then add the tomatoes to the dish, cover and microwave on full power until heated through and fragrant, about 3 minutes.

Scoop the tomato mixture into a processor or blender and whiz until combined. Add the tomato juice and tuna and process for about 30 seconds. Garnish with the olives and serve warm.

SPRING RENDEZVOUS

4 servings • 118 calories per serving

½ lb	asparagus, cleaned, peeled and chopped with tips reserved	225 g
1½ cups	watercress leaves	360 ml
5	scallions, chopped	
1 cup	baby peas	240 ml
2 Tbs	minced fresh thyme	30 ml
¼ cup	dry white wine or nonalcoholic wine	60 ml
1½ cups	buttermilk	360 ml
1 cup	milk	240 ml

Toss the asparagus into a 9-inch (23-cm) glass pie dish with the watercress, scallions, peas, thyme and wine. Cover with vented plastic wrap and microwave on full power until the vegetables are tender, about 4 minutes. Stir or shake midway.

Rinse the asparagus tips and toss into a small bowl. Cover with vented plastic wrap and microwave on full power for about 1 minute.

Meanwhile, scoop the vegetable mixture into a processor or blender and whiz until smooth and combined. Process or stir in the buttermilk and milk and serve garnished with asparagus tips.

GARLIC SOUP GRATINÉ

A no-salt-added alternative to traditional onion soup.

4 servings • 186 calories per serving

15	cloves garlic	
3	scallions	
2	shallots	
3	bay leaves	
½ tsp	sage	2 ml
1 cup	chicken stock	240 ml
2 cups	chicken stock	480 ml
1 cup	light cream or milk	240 ml
4	rounds of stale bread	
	grated Swiss cheese for sprinkling	

Combine the garlic, scallions, shallots, bay leaves, sage and 1 cup (240 ml) of stock in a 9-inch (23-cm) glass pie dish. Cover with vented plastic wrap and microwave on full power until the garlic is tender, about 5 minutes. Discard the bay leaves.

Pour the garlic mixture into a processor or blender and whiz until smooth. Process or stir in 2 cups (480 ml) of stock and the cream or milk.

Preheat the broiler and meanwhile, set the stale bread rounds in the bottoms of 4 individual, crocklike soup dishes. Pour in the soup, sprinkle with the grated Swiss and run under the broiler until golden, about 2 minutes. Serve hot.

SHRIMP AND SMOKED SALMON BISQUE

4 servings • 161 calories per serving

4 oz	smoked salmon, minced	110 g
1	onion, minced	
½ lb	shrimp, peeled and minced	225 g
2 Tbs	lemon juice	30 ml
¼ cup	chicken stock	60 ml
2 tsp	sweet butter	10 ml
3	scallions, chopped	
1½ cups	chicken stock, room temperature	360 ml
½ cup	light cream or milk	120 ml

Combine the salmon, onions, shrimp, lemon juice, ¼ cup (60 ml) stock and butter in a 9-inch (23-cm) glass pie dish. Cover with vented plastic wrap and microwave on full power for about 3 minutes.

Scoop the mixture, along with the scallions, into a processor or blender and whiz until smooth. Process or stir in 1½ cups (360 ml) stock and the cream or milk and serve warm.

Filé Facts

Filé (FEE-lay) is the dried ground root of the sassafras plant, and it is said that the best is dug up by the light of an August full moon. Filé is famous in Creole and Cajun cuisines, particularly in gumbos, and tastes sharp, green and vaguely thymelike. In fact, filé is often found mixed with thyme, and though the combination tastes good, it doesn't have the thickening powers of straight filé.

To use filé as a no-fat-added soup thickener, add about 1 teaspoon (5 ml) to 1 quart (1 liter) of just microwaved soup and let it stand for about 5 minutes. It's particularly nice with tomato-based soups.

CARROT SOUP WITH ROOTS AND TOPS

4 servings • 75 calories per serving

¾ lb	carrots, cut into even coins	340 g
2 Tbs	minced carrot tops or parsley	30 ml
1	onion, chopped	
1	shallot, chopped	
5	dried lemongrass straws or ½ tsp (2 ml) dried lemon peel	
1 tsp	sage	5 ml
¼ cup	chicken stock	60 ml
¾ cup	buttermilk	180 ml
1 cup	chicken stock, room temperature	240 ml

Combine the carrots, carrot tops or parsley, onions, shallots, lemongrass or lemon peel, sage and ¼ cup (60 ml) of stock in a 9-inch (23-cm) glass pie dish. Cover with vented plastic wrap and microwave on full power until the vegetables are tender, about 6 minutes. Stir or shake midway. Remove the lemongrass.

Scoop the carrot mixture into a processor or blender and whiz until smooth. Process or stir in the buttermilk and remaining 1 cup (240 ml) of stock and serve warm.

BROCCOLI PUREE WITH FENNEL AND PARMESAN

This is a light soup whose flair becomes more obvious as you eat it.

4 servings • 146 calories per serving

½ lb	broccoli, chopped	225 g
½ lb	cauliflower, chopped	225 g
3 oz	fennel bulb, chopped	85 g
2	shallots, chopped	
¼ cup	dry white wine or nonalcoholic wine	60 ml
1 Tbs	olive oil	15 ml
1 tsp	Dijon-style mustard	5 ml
½ cup	chicken stock, room temperature	120 ml
1 cup	milk	240 ml
	freshly grated Parmesan for sprinkling	

Combine the broccoli, cauliflower, fennel, shallots and wine in a 9-inch (23-cm) glass pie dish and cover with vented plastic wrap. Microwave on full power until the vegetables are tender, about 6 minutes, stirring or shaking midway. Let stand for 5 minutes.

Scoop the broccoli mixture into a processor or blender and whiz until smooth. Process or stir in the oil, mustard, stock and milk and serve warm or chilled, sprinkled with Parmesan.

COWBOY SOUP

Nice microwaved in a clay cooking pot.

4 servings • 145 calories per serving

Scoop the corn, scallions and onions into a processor or blender and whiz until smooth. Then transfer to a large, clay cooking pot or large, casserole-type dish and add the rest of the ingredients except the cheese. Cover and microwave until cooked through, about 6 minutes, stirring or shaking midway. Remove bay leaves and serve hot, sprinkled with Jack cheese.

⅔ cup	corn kernels	160 ml
1	scallion, chopped	
1	onion, chopped	
2 cups	crushed tomatoes	480 ml
1 cup	chicken stock	240 ml
1 Tbs	minced fresh coriander	15 ml
½ tsp	oregano	2 ml
½ tsp	hot, Mexican-type chili powder	2 ml
2	cloves garlic, minced	
1	jalapeño pepper, seeded and finely minced (wear plastic gloves when handling)	
2	bay leaves	
	grated Monterey Jack cheese for sprinkling	

LENTIL SOUP FROM THE SOUTH OF INDIA

Here's a fast-cooking example of **Rasan,** *an Indian lentil soup traditionally enjoyed before a feast. As you will see, it's actually a feast in itself.*

4 servings • 174 calories per serving

In a large, clay cooking pot or a large, casserole-type dish combine the curry powder, coriander, cumin, cardamom, chamomile, cayenne or other red pepper, orange peel, garlic and oil. Cover and microwave on full power until fragrant, about 2 minutes.

Next add the leeks, carrots, celery, bay leaf, lentils and stock. Cover and microwave on full power until the lentils are tender, about 25 minutes. Let the soup stand for 10 minutes, then remove bay leaf and serve hot.

1 tsp	curry powder	5 ml
½ tsp	coriander seeds, ground	2 ml
¼ tsp	cumin seeds, ground	1 ml
	seeds of 1 cardamom pod, ground	
½ tsp	dried chamomile, ground	2 ml
pinch	cayenne pepper or other ground red pepper	
¼ tsp	freshly grated orange peel	1 ml
2	cloves garlic, minced	
1 Tbs	peanut oil	15 ml
1	leek, finely minced	
1	carrot, finely minced	
1	stalk celery, leaves too, finely minced	
1	bay leaf	
⅔ cup	lentils	160 ml
4 cups	chicken stock	1 liter

MUSHROOM LOVER'S SOUP

4 servings • 97 calories per serving

¼ lb	mushrooms, chopped	110 g
1 tsp	sweet butter	5 ml
2 cups	chicken stock	480 ml
1 to 5	large, dried porcini mushrooms, rinsed and cut into pieces, optional	
3	scallions, chopped	
2 Tbs	minced fresh parsley	30 ml
1	shallot, chopped	
¼ tsp	tarragon	1 ml
1 cup	cooked rice	240 ml
½ cup	milk	120 ml
1 tsp	freshly squeezed lemon juice	5 ml
	thinly sliced mushrooms for garnishing	

Toss the chopped mushrooms and butter into a large, casserole-type dish. Cover and microwave on full power for 50 seconds, stirring midway.

Add the stock, mushroom pieces (if using), scallions, parsley, shallots and tarragon to the dish. Cover with vented plastic wrap and microwave on full power for 4½ to 5 minutes. Let stand for 5 minutes.

Pour the mixture into a processor or blender and whiz until smooth, adding the rice, milk and lemon juice while the motor is still running. Serve immediately, garnished with mushroom slices.

JANUARY SOUP

Serve this when you've had all you can take of rich holiday foods. It's fragrant and delicious and a strictly no-fat-added soup.

4 servings • 88 calories per serving

Combine all of the ingredients in a clay cooking pot or a casserole-type dish, cover and microwave on full power until the vegetables are tender and fragrant, about 10 minutes. Let stand for 5 minutes, then remove bay leaves and serve hot.

1	carrot, finely minced	
1	parsnip, finely minced	
1	turnip, finely minced	
1	leek, cleaned and finely minced	
1	small (not pearl) onion, finely minced	
3	bay leaves	
3	dried porcini mushrooms, finely minced	
1½ cups	chicken stock	360 ml
½ cup	dry white wine or nonalcoholic wine	120 ml

THAI LEMONGRASS SOUP WITH SHRIMP AND SCALLIONS

Nam pla *is to Thai food what soy sauce is to Chinese. It's less salty than most soy sauces and is available at Oriental markets and specialty foods stores. It's also called* **nuoc nam** *in Vietnamese cooking.*

4 servings • 42 calories per serving

3 cups	chicken stock	720 ml
2 tsp	*nam pla* or light soy sauce	10 ml
splash	hot pepper sauce	
handful	dried lemongrass or 2 tsp (10 ml) dried lemon peel	
1 Tbs	minced fresh basil	15 ml
1 Tbs	minced fresh mint	15 ml
4 oz	shrimp, peeled and halved vertically	110 g
3	scallions, cut into fine julienne	

Combine the stock, *nam pla* or soy sauce, hot pepper sauce, lemongrass or dried lemon peel, basil and mint in a large, clay cooking pot or a large, casserole-type dish, cover and microwave until heated through and fragrant, about 7 minutes. Let stand while you prepare the shrimp.

Set the shrimp around the rim of a large plate. Cover with vented plastic wrap and microwave on full power until the shrimp are pink and firm but not rubbery, about 2 minutes. Meanwhile, fish the lemongrass out of the soup and discard.

Add the shrimp to the soup, along with the scallions, and serve hot.

LEMON MISO SOUP WITH VEGETABLE JULIENNE AND SKINNY NOODLES

4 servings • 133 calories per serving

In a large, casserole-type dish combine the water, tea bags, leeks, parsnips, celery, carrots, miso and bay leaves. Cover and microwave on full power until the vegetables are tender, about 5 minutes.

Remove and discard the tea bags and bay leaves. Add the stock, noodles, chives and oils and serve hot.

2 cups	water	480 ml
2	lemon-hibiscus herbal-type tea bags, tags removed	
1	leek, cut into fine julienne	
1	parsnip, cut into fine julienne	
1	celery stalk, cut into fine julienne	
1	small carrot, cut into fine julienne	
2 tsp	miso	10 ml
3	bay leaves	
1 cup	hot chicken stock	240 ml
1 cup	cooked skinny noodles	240 ml
¼ cup	minced fresh chives	60 ml
2 tsp	toasted sesame oil	10 ml
splash	chili oil	

ICY CUKE SOUP

4 servings • 93 calories per serving

In a large, casserole-type dish combine the cucumbers, scallions, garlic, dillweed, mint and stock. Cover and microwave on full power until the cukes are tender, about 5 minutes. Let stand for 2 minutes, then pour into a processor or blender and whiz until smooth.

Chill the mixture and when you're ready to serve, fold in the yogurt, lemon juice and lemon peel. Garnish with mint sprigs.

4	medium cucumbers, peeled, seeded and chopped	
3	scallions, chopped	
1	clove garlic, chopped	
½ tsp	dillweed	2 ml
¼ tsp	mint	1 ml
1 cup	beef stock	240 ml
1 cup	plain, low-fat yogurt	240 ml
1 Tbs	freshly squeezed lemon juice	15 ml
pinch	freshly grated lemon peel	
	sprigs fresh mint for garnishing	

CREAMY PEACH SOUP

For a light entrée, serve with crisp greens and a bread and cheese platter. The soup is good warm, fabulous chilled.

4 servings • 219 calories per serving

3½ cups	very ripe peaches, peeled, pitted and sliced	840 ml
⅓ cup	dry white wine or nonalcoholic wine	80 ml
¼ cup	strawberry jam	60 ml
2 tsp	sweet butter	10 ml
½ cup	light cream, milk or buttermilk	120 ml
	freshly grated nutmeg for sprinkling	
	fresh strawberries or raspberries for garnishing, optional	

In a large, casserole-type dish combine the peaches, wine, jam and butter. Cover and microwave on full power until heated through, about 3 minutes. Then pour the mixture into a processor or blender and whiz until smooth. Process or stir in the cream or milk and serve warm or chilled, sprinkled with the nutmeg. If you wish, garnish with strawberries or raspberries.

FROM
THE GARDEN

In a sense, the microwave of today is somewhat like the refrigerator of the past. Both were welcomed enthusiastically. Each offered a new convenience and each changed the way we incorporate vegetables into our diet. Refrigeration, of course, gave us a chance to store fresh produce from around the country and eventually around the globe. Microwaves have given us the opportunity to prepare that produce in record time.

Speedy cooking is appreciated in a busy schedule, and it's also a big health plus. If vegetables are microwaved, then cooking time is reduced, which in turn reduces the loss of heat-sensitive nutrients. And because microwaving vegetables requires less liquid than conventional cooking, fewer nutrients are washed away. Microwaving also encourages cooks to prepare in minutes nutrient-dense vegetables that traditionally require long cooking.

In fact, for superior taste, texture and color, microwaving may be the best cooking method for long-cooking produce like squash, sweet potatoes, turnips, parsnips and eggplant. The truth is, I actually prefer squash and eggplant when microwaved. Their textures are consistently silky and their tastes are striking and delicious. Kohlrabi is another made-for-microwave vegetable. Its skin slips easily from its flesh revealing toothsome chunks of sweet, hardy vegetable. Microwaving also makes short order of fresh pumpkin for pies and purees. The process is so easy and the outcome so successful you'll think twice before opening a can. Even pumpkin seeds, formerly a real pain to roast, can be prepared in a snap in the microwave.

Long-cooking or otherwise, vegetables cooked in a microwave taste good. For years we overcooked vegetables to bland mush. Then in protest we undercooked vegetables to a crispness that belonged more at a picnic than at the dinner table. Now, with microwaving, we can have gently cooked textures and still retain fresh tastes and aromas. Microwaved vegetables are bold and true and require few frills. Imagine steaming hot, sweetly fragrant carrots. It would be unthinkable to restrain their elegance by dousing them with salt and a heavy cream sauce. Instead, toss them with crushed fresh herbs and a splash of fruity olive oil.

Microwaving vegetables is a technique with few but important rules. To begin with, always use the freshest, best-looking produce you can find. Microwaving won't hide flaws so if you try to cook some tired old peas, for instance, you're going to end up with tired old peas.

Also, vegetables should be cut in equal-size pieces so that all will cook at the same time. Also, for even cooking, if you're mixing vegetables, mix similar-textured ones. Carrots and parsnips are a good match but carrots and peas are not because the peas could overcook. You can, however, start cooking the carrots and add the peas later.

If one vegetable has two textures, like asparagus spears and tips or broccoli stalks and florets, arrange the vegetables in a starburst pattern with the tender textures (tips and florets) at the center.

As for cookware, a round, shallow container, like a 9-inch (23-cm) microwave-safe pie dish, will help most vegetables cook evenly. The pie dish can be covered with vented plastic wrap or crumpled waxed paper, depending on the vegetable you're cooking and the results you want.

Be sure to stir or shake the vegetables every two minutes or so, even if you have a turntable or wave baffler. This will help guarantee even cooking.

SWEET POTATO SALAD WITH PEANUT DRESSING

4 servings • 183 calories per serving

Combine the sweet potato chunks and stock in a 9-inch (23-cm) glass pie dish and cover with vented plastic wrap. Microwave on full power for about 6 minutes, stirring every 2 minutes. Let stand, covered, for 5 minutes.

Meanwhile, make the dressing by combining the maple syrup, lemon juice, oil, shallots and peanuts in a small bowl. If necessary, drain the sweet potato chunks before tossing them with the dressing. Serve warm or chilled.

1 lb	sweet potatoes, cut into 1- × 2-inch (2.5- × 5-cm) chunks	450 g
3 Tbs	chicken stock	45 ml
½ tsp	maple syrup	2 ml
2 Tbs	freshly squeezed lemon juice	30 ml
1 Tbs	peanut oil	15 ml
1	shallot, finely minced	
¼ cup	crushed, toasted peanuts	60 ml

Variation: Add 2 tsp (10 ml) of minced fresh coriander to the dressing.

CHINESE VEGETABLES WITH SESAME GARNISH

This is a good way to use a browning dish to cook vegetables. If you don't have one, use a 9-inch (23-cm) microwave-safe pie dish. Cover the vegetables loosely with waxed paper and microwave on full power for about 4 minutes.

4 servings • 53 calories per serving

Preheat a browning dish for 5 minutes if it's nonstick and 4 minutes if it's not.

In a large bowl, combine the mushrooms, cabbage and bok choy ribs. In a small bowl, whisk together the soy sauce, honey, ginger and garlic and toss to combine with the vegetables.

When the browning dish is ready, paint the surface with a bit of peanut oil if it's not a nonstick dish. Scoop on the vegetables and lay a sheet of waxed paper over them. Microwave on full power for 2 minutes, stirring midway.

While the vegetables are still hot, toss in with the bok choy leaves, scallions, sesame seeds and oil and serve. The combination is wonderful with steaming rice or skinny Chinese noodles.

2 oz	button mushrooms, sliced	60 g
7 oz	cabbage, sliced into shreds	200 g
5	bok choy ribs, cut into ½-inch (2-cm) slices	
2 tsp	light soy sauce	10 ml
1 tsp	honey	5 ml
¼ tsp	minced fresh ginger	1 ml
1	clove garlic, minced	
	peanut oil for painting, if necessary	
¼ cup	shredded bok choy leaves	60 ml
2	scallions, minced	
1 Tbs	toasted sesame seeds	15 ml
1 tsp	sesame oil	5 ml

A Toast for Peanuts

To toast crushed peanuts, lay a sheet of waxed paper on the floor of your microwave. Spread out ¼ cup (60 ml) of crushed peanuts and microwave, uncovered, on full power for about 5 minutes, stirring every minute. This aromatic, no-fat-added method makes tasty sprinkles for cooked green beans, eggplant, broccoli, parsnips and squash.

ONIONS
IN A BAG

This is an exciting variation on stewed onions and the cleanup is a lot easier. You'll need an oven cooking bag, but don't use the tie that comes with it.

The onions, which incidentally are reputed to be good for the heart, are even more delicious when reheated the second day.

4 servings • 69 calories per serving

4	medium onions, peeled and quartered	
1 Tbs	flour	15 ml
3	tomatoes, peeled, seeded and chopped, including juice	
1	clove garlic, minced	
½ tsp	sage	2 ml
½ tsp	basil	2 ml
1 Tbs	minced celery leaves	15 ml
¼ cup	chicken stock	60 ml
½ cup	cooked black beans	120 ml

Toss the onions into the oven cooking bag along with the flour, tomatoes, garlic, sage, basil, celery and stock. Mix the ingredients around, making sure the flour is incorporated. Tie a knot in the bag. Repeat: Don't use the tie that comes with it. Poke a few air holes in the bag, using the sharp tines of a fork. Set the bag on a plate to make it easier to handle, and microwave for about 5 minutes on full power, rearranging the onions midway without opening the bag. Let the onions stand for about 3 minutes before opening the bag to serve. Scoop the onions into a bowl and stir in the black beans.

A Toast for Sesame Seeds

To toast sesame seeds in a microwave, preheat an ungreased browning dish for about 2½ minutes. Sprinkle on 1 tablespoon (15 ml) of sesame seeds, cover them loosely with waxed paper and microwave on full power for about 1½ minutes, shaking every 30 seconds during cooking. Watch them attentively because they can burn quickly. If you don't have a browning dish, use a 9-inch (23-cm) glass pie dish, cover loosely with waxed paper and microwave on full power for 2½ to 3 minutes. They're a rich, crunchy sprinkle for asparagus, carrots and squash, and contain fewer calories than many nuts.

BRAISED FENNEL WITH PARMESAN AND RIPE TOMATOES

This is an especially nice accompaniment to fish. If the fennel is at all old and tough, peel it before cutting into pieces.

4 servings • 53 calories per serving

1 lb	fennel, trimmed and cut into 1-inch (2.5-cm) pieces	450 g
¼ cup	chicken stock	60 ml
1 tsp	celery seeds	5 ml
1	bay leaf	
2	cloves garlic, minced	
½ tsp	thyme	2 ml
2	ripe tomatoes, chopped and drained	
3 Tbs	freshly grated Parmesan	45 ml

Toss the fennel into a 9-inch (23-cm) glass pie dish along with the stock, celery seeds, bay leaf, garlic and thyme and combine well. Cover with vented plastic wrap and microwave on full power for 4½ to 5 minutes, stirring or shaking midway. Let stand for 3 minutes, drain without losing the garlic, toss with the tomatoes and Parmesan. Remove bay leaf and serve.

Skewered Vegetables

Mushroom caps, pearl onions, zucchini chunks and eggplant cubes are great for microwave kabobs. Be sure to use vegetables that are similar in texture and size and marinate them in freshly squeezed lemon juice, olive oil and an aromatic, like thyme. Thread the vegetables on 6-inch (15-cm) bamboo skewers and set the skewers along the rim of a large, flat plate. Cover with vented plastic wrap and microwave on full power for 4 to 4½ minutes per pound (450 g) of vegetables, rotating the skewers midway. Let the skewers stand for about 3 minutes before serving with poached chicken or fish.

Broccoli Basics

To cook 1 pound (450 g) of fresh broccoli florets, set the rinsed, still-wet florets into a 9-inch (23-cm) microwave-safe pie dish and cover with vented plastic wrap. Then microwave on full power for 4½ to 5 minutes, shaking or stirring every 2 minutes. Let the florets stand for 3 minutes before serving. Cauliflower can be cooked the same way.

Chopped broccoli that contains some stalk will take a bit longer, especially if the stalk is tough. Peeling the stalk before chopping cuts the cooking time and helps the florets and stalks to cook more evenly together.

Whole spears of broccoli with florets attached should be arranged, while still wet, on a flat plate in a starburst pattern with the florets at the center to protect their more delicate texture. The spears should be covered with vented plastic wrap. One pound (450 g) will take about 5 minutes to microwave on full power and should be rotated midway. Then let the spears stand for about 3 minutes before serving.

Ideas for Flavorings

Toss with warm florets or sprinkle over spears:

- Splash of olive oil, minced sweet red peppers and freshly ground black pepper
- Dijon-style mustard and a pinch of tarragon
- Dash of toasted sesame oil, toasted sesame seeds and minced scallions
- Splash of peanut oil, minced scallions, crushed peanuts and cooked rice
- Plain, low-fat yogurt and a dash of prepared horseradish
- Cooked corn kernels, minced chives and a splash of olive oil
- Chopped ripe tomatoes and a pinch of oregano

Microwaving Cactus Pads

These are also called *nopales** and are the leaves of the prickly pear cactus. They look like flat, green mittens without the thumbs, weigh about 3 ounces (85 g) apiece and are high in vitamins A and C.

They taste like tart green beans and have sort of an okralike texture. Toss cooked cactus pads with spicy tomato salsa or a garlic vinaigrette and serve with Mexican food.

To microwave one pad, peel with a paring knife or swivel-bladed vegetable peeler. Be careful of the thorns. Slice into strips, toss into a 9-inch (23-cm) glass pie dish with a tablespoon of chicken stock or water and cover with vented plastic wrap. Microwave on full power for 1 minute and let stand for 1 minute more.

*Available in Spanish markets and many supermarkets.

TINY WHOLE CARROTS WITH MUSTARD AND CHERVIL

If you don't have baby carrots, use larger ones cut into 2- × ½-inch (5- × 1-cm) bâtons. The important thing is that they're all the same size or they won't cook evenly.

4 servings • 65 calories per serving

¾ lb	baby carrots, washed and peeled with tops attached	340 g
2 Tbs	chicken stock	30 ml
2 tsp	peanut oil	10 ml
2 tsp	Dijon-style mustard	10 ml
2 Tbs	freshly squeezed orange juice	30 ml
1 Tbs	minced fresh chervil or flat-leaf parsley	15 ml

Combine the carrots and stock in a 9-inch (23-cm) glass pie dish and cover with vented plastic wrap. Microwave on full power for 6½ to 7 minutes, stirring or shaking a couple of times during cooking. Let stand for 3 minutes.

Meanwhile, in a small bowl, combine the peanut oil, mustard, orange juice and chervil or parsley. When the carrots are ready, drain them. Toss the carrots with the mustard and chervil sauce or use the sauce as a dip.

Note: The sauce is also great with cooked cauliflower.

The Wet-Towel Carrot Trick

Carrots can be easily cooked in wet paper towels. Simply stack three towels together and wet them with water. Squeeze out slightly, then lay them out flat. Set ½ pound (225 g) of thinly sliced carrot coins in the center of the towels, sprinkle with dill and close the towels up like an envelope. Set the package on a plate so it's easier to handle, and microwave on full power for about 4 minutes, rotating the package once during cooking. Let stand for about 3 minutes before serving.

Spicy Indian Sauce
(Chonk)

This is a sizzling mixture of spices from India that's added to food just before serving. Traditionally the spices are sizzled in oil or **ghee,** *but this leaner version sizzles mostly in stock. The spices here resemble an Indian curry but you may vary the concept to suit your taste. Have ready 1 pound (450 g) of just-cooked vegetables like zucchini, green beans, potatoes, shell beans, turnips, carrots, cauliflower or onions.*

4 servings • 16 calories per serving

½ tsp	coriander seeds, ground	2 ml
¼ tsp	cumin seeds, ground	1 ml
pinch	white mustard seeds, ground	
¼ tsp	turmeric	1 ml
	seeds of 3 cardamom pods, ground	
pinch	cayenne pepper or other ground red pepper	
1	bay leaf, crumbled	
1	clove garlic, finely minced	
¼ cup	chicken stock	60 ml
1 tsp	sweet butter	5 ml
½ tsp	honey	2 ml

Combine all of the ingredients in a small bowl, cover with vented plastic wrap and microwave on full power for about 1 minute. Let stand for about 4 minutes so the flavors can blend, then toss with warm vegetables.

Green Bean Cuisine

For best texture and color, green beans should be cut into pieces before microwaving. Half-inch (1-cm) pieces work well and can be cut on a severe diagonal to make them more interesting. Young, tender green beans will give you the best results. Toss 1 pound (450 g) of rinsed, still-wet green bean pieces into a microwave-safe dish, cover and microwave on full power for about 4½ minutes. Let them stand for 3 minutes before serving.

Ideas for Flavorings

Toss with warm green beans:

- Freshly squeezed lemon juice and a pinch of summer savory
- Splash of olive oil, sunflower seeds and finely minced purple onions
- Chili sauce, finely minced scallions and finely minced celery
- Toasted bread crumbs, grated mozzarella, finely minced sweet onions and a pinch of oregano
- Splash of sesame oil, splash of hot chili oil and a pinch each of finely minced fresh ginger and garlic

Recipe Conversion Tip

When converting a conventional vegetable recipe to a microwave one, you can reduce the amount of butter or oil because vegetables won't stick in a microwave.

STUFFED WHOLE ONIONS

The stuffing here is a fragrant combination of mustard and autumn offerings, but you can vary the idea to suit your taste. You can even stuff the onions with ground meat, but be sure to cook it first.

4 servings • 105 calories per serving

4	medium onions	
1	apple, grated and drained	
2 Tbs	minced raisins	30 ml
2 Tbs	toasted, unsalted sunflower seeds	30 ml
pinch	freshly grated nutmeg	
1 tsp	Dijon-style mustard	5 ml
2 Tbs	chicken stock	30 ml
2 Tbs	apple juice	30 ml
¼ cup	grated cheddar	60 ml

Use a melon baller to scoop out as much pulp from the onions as possible while still leaving strong shells. Mince about a third of the onion scoopings (save the rest to flavor other recipes) and combine with the apples, raisins, sunflower seeds, nutmeg and mustard. Stuff the whole onions with the mixture and set them in a high-sided dish. Pour in the stock and apple juice, cover and microwave on full power for about 5 minutes, rotating the onions midway.

Remove the cover and sprinkle the onions with the grated cheddar. Let them stand for about 5 minutes before serving.

Even Cooking for Brussels Sprouts

If your microwaved Brussels sprouts have been less than great, try this: For 1 pound (450 g) of sprouts, trim the stem ends slightly, then carve an "×" in each. Combine the sprouts with 2 tablespoons (30 ml) of chicken stock or water in a 9-inch (23-cm) glass pie dish, cover with vented plastic wrap and microwave on full power for 6 to 8 minutes. Let them stand for about 3 minutes before serving.

JICAMA BÂTONS WITH CUMIN AND LIME

A refreshing partner to refried beans and spicy tomato salsa.

4 servings • 86 calories per serving

Combine the jicama, peppers, garlic, lime juice, hot pepper sauce, oregano, olive oil, maple syrup and cumin in a 9-inch (23-cm) glass pie dish and cover with

1 lb	jicama, sliced into thin, 3-inch (8-cm) bâtons	450 g
1	sweet red pepper, minced	
2	cloves garlic, finely minced	
¼ cup	freshly squeezed lime juice	60 ml
5	drops hot pepper sauce, or to taste	
½ tsp	oregano	2 ml
2 tsp	olive oil	10 ml
1 tsp	maple syrup	5 ml
1 tsp	cumin seeds, ground	5 ml
1 Tbs	minced fresh chives	15 ml

vented plastic wrap. Microwave on full power for about 4 minutes, then let stand for 2 minutes more. If the jicama flesh is particularly hard and dense, you'll need to cook it longer. Begin with a 30-second increase and add more time if necessary. Generally, the bigger the jicama, the tougher it will be.

Chill the jicama mixture for at least an hour, toss with the chives and serve.

Chestnuts, for a Change

Cooked chestnuts have a texture like chickpeas and taste like rich sweet potatoes. Chop and add them to stuffings for poultry or toss with cooked Chinese peas, sweet potatoes, broccoli or green beans. They're also a wonderful garnish for cream soups, poached chicken, fruit salads and greens.

To microwave chestnuts, combine ½ pound (225 g) of chestnuts with ¼ cup (60 ml) of water in a microwave-safe dish. Cover and microwave on full power for about 4½ minutes, stirring or shaking midway. Then let them stand until cool enough to handle, about 5 minutes, and peel the chestnuts with a paring knife.

GARLIC PUREE WITH RICOTTA

Serve with still-warm broccoli or potatoes, with roast meats or poultry, grilled fish, warm shrimp, and raw vegetable platters or as a spread for crusty bread.

12	cloves garlic, mashed	
½ cup	chicken stock	120 ml
1	bay leaf	
2 Tbs	ricotta cheese	30 ml

Makes about ⅓ cup • 113 calories per serving

In a 9-inch (23-cm) glass pie dish, combine the garlic, stock and bay leaf and cover with vented plastic wrap. Microwave on full power until the garlic is tender, about 6½ minutes. Let stand for 4 minutes more.

Remove the bay leaf and dump the garlic and stock into a processor or blender. Whiz until smooth, adding the ricotta while the motor is running. Serve room temperature or chilled.

Cassava Instead of Potatoes

This is the stem of the yucca plant, and it's also called *manioc*. The stem is peeled, cooked and eaten like white potatoes, although cassava's texture is more fibrous. Cassava is popular in Brazilian, West Indian and other Caribbean cuisines and can be found fresh or frozen in Hispanic markets and many supermarkets.

Apart from its culinary appeal, cassava is gaining applause from people with arthritis, as a potato substitute. Unlike potatoes, cassava contains no solanine, a substance suspected of aggravating arthritis.

To microwave cassava, chop 1 pound (450 g) into equal-size pieces and toss them into a 9-inch (23-cm) glass pie dish with 2 tablespoons (30 ml) of chicken stock. Cover with vented plastic wrap and microwave on full power for about 4½ minutes, stirring or shaking midway. Let stand for 3 minutes.

Mash the cooked cassava with a potato masher or large fork, but don't use a processor or blender because the texture will be too gummy. Add about 3 tablespoons (45 ml) of milk, a pinch each of oregano and ground allspice and a bit of sweet butter. If your microwave has browning capability, use it to give the mashed cassava a bit of color. Otherwise, run the cassava under a broiler until speckled with gold. Serve with roast pork or stews of tropical origin.

PUREE OF WINTER SQUASH WITH ROSEMARY

The flavor in this recipe is dependent on the best-quality, freshest squash available. Generally, the more vivid the color of the flesh, the more flavorful the squash. If you cut yours open to find a paleface, augment its flavor by adding some carrots or sweet potatoes.

4 servings • 66 calories per serving

1 lb	winter squash, like butternut, peeled, seeded and cut into 1-inch (2.5-cm) chunks	450 g
½ cup	chicken stock	120 ml
¾ tsp	rosemary	3 ml
2 tsp	sweet butter	10 ml

Toss the squash, the stock and the rosemary into a 9-inch (23-cm) glass pie dish and cover with vented plastic wrap. Microwave on full power for about 5 minutes and let stand for 3 minutes more. Scoop the squash and rosemary and about 3 Tbs (45 ml) of the stock into a processor or blender and puree until smooth, adding the butter while the motor is running. Serve warm with roast turkey, pheasant or other poultry.

Squash for One

Wrap half of a 1-pound (450-g), seeded acorn or butternut squash in waxed paper and microwave on full power for about 3½ minutes. Let it stand for 3 minutes more. Fill with pasta salad, marinated vegetables or greens. For breakfast, fill with vanilla yogurt and sprinkle with chopped pecans.

BUTTERNUT SQUASH WITH CIDER CREAM

Flavorful pumpkin can substitute for the squash.

4 servings • 73 calories per serving

1 lb	butternut squash, peeled, seeded and cut into 1-inch (2.5-cm) chunks	450 g
3 Tbs	chicken stock	45 ml
⅓ cup	plain, low-fat yogurt	80 ml
2 tsp	maple syrup, or to taste	10 ml
3 Tbs	apple cider or apple juice	45 ml
dash	freshly grated nutmeg	

Toss the squash and the stock into a 9-inch (23-cm) glass pie dish, cover and microwave on full power for about 4 minutes. Let stand 5 minutes more, then drain.

Meanwhile, in a small bowl, combine the yogurt, maple syrup, cider or apple juice and nutmeg. Toss with the squash and serve warm.

Easier Cutting for Squash

If you're wrestling with a winter squash or pumpkin that's too hard to cut, wrap the whole thing in waxed paper and microwave. A 1-pound (450-g) squash microwaved on full power for about 2 minutes will be much easier to cut.

A Toast for Squash or Pumpkin Seeds

When microwaving squash or pumpkin seeds, omit the oil you'd use when roasting them conventionally. For example, scoop the seeds from one squash, about ½ cup (120 ml), rinse well or they'll stick, and pat dry. Then lay the seeds out on waxed paper set on a plate for easy handling and microwave on full power, uncovered, for about 5 minutes. Stir or shake every minute and watch them carefully because they could burn or cook unevenly. Sprinkle the seeds with chili powder or curry powder and let them stand for an additional 3 minutes. Enjoy as a snack or a garnish for greens or carrot soup.

BRAISED LEEKS WITH WARM TOMATO VINAIGRETTE

The vinaigrette is also delicious with cooked asparagus, zucchini slices, carrot bâtons, broccoli, green and wax beans and cold poached chicken and fish.

4 servings • 144 calories per serving

4	large leeks	
3 Tbs	chicken stock	45 ml
1	medium, ripe tomato	
2 Tbs	red wine vinegar	30 ml
1 Tbs	olive oil	15 ml
2 Tbs	chicken stock	30 ml
1	clove garlic, minced	

Clean the leeks under running water, removing all their sand. Slice off the roots and tough green ends. Then slice each leek in half vertically, taking care not to disrupt the petal formation. Set the leeks cut side down in a starburst pattern with the white parts at the center, in a 9-inch (23-cm) glass pie dish. Sprinkle with the 3 Tbs (45 ml) of stock and cover with vented plastic wrap. Microwave on full power for 4½ to 5 minutes or until the leeks are tender, rotating the dish midway. Let them stand while you prepare the vinaigrette.

In a processor or blender combine the tomato, vinegar, oil, remaining stock and garlic and whiz until well combined. When you're ready to serve, pour the vinaigrette into a small bowl, cover with plastic wrap and microwave on full power for about 5 seconds, or until warm. Then pour it in a pool onto a serving plate and set the leeks in, cut side down.

Recipe Conversion Tip

To cut fat and calories, microwave chopped onions instead of sautéing them. Scoop ¼ cup (60 ml) into a small bowl and cover with vented plastic wrap. Microwave on full power for about 3 minutes, stirring or shaking midway. Use whenever sautéed onions are required.

Onions in a Bag (page 82)

Tiny Whole Carrots with Mustard and Chervil (page 85)

Puree of Winter Squash with Rosemary (page 90)

Marinated Sweet Peppers (page 101)

Red Snapper with Jalapeño Butter (page 113)

Chilled Haddock with Snow Peas and Orange Vinaigrette (page 132)

Flounder Mosaics (page 133)

Shrimp in a Bamboo Steamer (page 134)

MARINATED SWEET PEPPERS

Serve with pasta, omelettes or frittatas.

4 servings • 104 calories per serving

Slice the tops off the peppers and scrape out the seeds and ribs with a spoon. Cut each pepper into 6 thick slices and toss into a 9-inch (23-cm) glass pie dish with the stock. Cover with vented plastic wrap and microwave on full power for about 4½ minutes, stirring or shaking midway. Let the peppers stand for 2 minutes.

Meanwhile, in a medium bowl, combine the vinegar, scallions, garlic, marjoram, thyme, mustard, oil, capers and tomatoes. When the peppers are ready, drain them and toss into the marinade. Combine well, cover, and let marinate overnight in the refrigerator. The peppers will keep, refrigerated, for about a week.

4	sweet peppers, red, yellow or green	
2 Tbs	chicken stock	30 ml
¼ cup	champagne vinegar or white wine vinegar	60 ml
2	scallions, finely minced	
2	cloves garlic, finely minced	
½ tsp	marjoram	2 ml
½ tsp	thyme	2 ml
1 tsp	Dijon-style mustard	5 ml
1 Tbs	olive oil	15 ml
1 tsp	minced capers	5 ml
2	medium tomatoes, sliced into wedges	

Peeling Tomatoes

To peel a tomato in the microwave, carve an "X" in the skin of the stem end. Then wrap the tomato in waxed paper and microwave for 1 minute. Small, ripe tomatoes will take less time than large, underripe ones.

Let the tomato stand until cool enough to handle, about a minute, then peel off the skin with a paring knife.

ASPARAGUS WITH THYME AND ORANGE BUTTER

Usually, there's no need to peel asparagus in conventional cooking. When asparagus is microwaved, it tends to get pruney if the peels are left intact.

1 lb	asparagus	450 g
2 tsp	sweet butter	10 ml
¼ tsp	grated orange peel	1 ml
pinch	thyme	

4 servings • 47 calories per serving

Hold each asparagus spear in both hands and snap off the tough part. Then use a swivel-bladed vegetable peeler to peel the spears, leaving on a slice of peel here and there for color. Arrange the spears on a flat plate in a starburst design with the tender tips at the center. Cover with vented plastic wrap and microwave on full power for 4 to 5 minutes, depending on the thickness and toughness of the spears. Let them stand for 2 minutes.

Meanwhile, combine the butter, orange peel and thyme in a small bowl, cover with vented plastic wrap and microwave on full power until the butter is melted, about 40 seconds. Toss the asparagus with the butter and serve warm or room temperature.

Easier Cooking for Shell Beans

These are the middle stage of bean life, the first being similar to the green beans we know, and the last being dried beans. Shell beans are most common in the spring and a familiar type is the fresh (as opposed to dry) cranberry bean.

To microwave 1 pound (450 g) of shell beans, toss them into a deep-sided dish with ⅔ cup (160 ml) of chicken stock and a bay leaf. Cover and microwave on full power for 5 to 7 minutes, or until the beans are tender, stirring or shaking every 2 minutes. Favas, another famous shell bean, will take longer to cook than smaller beans. Regardless of the variety, let the beans stand for about 5 minutes, drain, remove bay leaf and serve.

Ideas for Flavorings

Toss with warm shell beans, cooked dried beans or cooked black-eye peas:

- Rice vinegar, a splash of peanut oil, minced shallots and minced fresh mint
- Chopped plum tomatoes, minced green chili peppers, minced garlic, oregano and a splash of olive oil
- Steamed florets of cauliflower and broccoli, minced fresh, flat-leaf parsley, minced garlic, a splash of olive oil and freshly grated Romano cheese
- Cooked tiny pasta (like orzo), lemon juice, thyme, minced shallots and shredded spinach
- Chopped cooked shrimp, minced sweet peppers, a pinch of marjoram and a splash of olive oil

Great-Tasting Kohlrabi Globes

Begin with kohlrabies that are no larger than 3 inches in diameter. To microwave 1 pound (450 g), snip off the roots and stems, then quarter. Toss the quarters into a 9-inch (23-cm) glass pie dish and add 3 tablespoons chicken stock. Cover with vented plastic wrap and microwave on full power for about 7 minutes, stirring or shaking every 2 minutes. Let the kohlrabies stand for 5 minutes, or until cool enough to handle. To peel, slip a paring knife between the skin and flesh and pull down. The skin will zip right off.

Ideas for Flavorings

Toss with warm kohlrabies:

- Dijon-style mustard, a splash of half-and-half and a pinch of ground nutmeg
- Minced fresh dill and a splash of olive oil
- Finely minced celery, finely minced scallions and a pinch of ground caraway seeds

Kohlrabi globes are also delicious in place of potatoes in potato salad recipes. The leaves may be used in place of spinach or bok choy leaves, kale, collards or mustard greens.

JAPANESE EGGPLANT SALAD

Japanese eggplant, called ai gwa *or* nasube, *is thinner than western eggplant and comes in wonderful shades of ivory and lilac. You may use western eggplant in this recipe but the cooking time will be slightly longer.*

4 servings • 59 calories per serving

1 lb	Japanese eggplant or regular, halved vertically peanut oil for rubbing	450 g
1 Tbs	rice vinegar	15 ml
1 tsp	light soy sauce	5 ml
1 tsp	peanut butter	5 ml
½ tsp	honey	2 ml
splash	sesame oil	
2	scallions, minced	
1 Tbs	toasted sesame seeds	15 ml

Rub the cut sides of the eggplant with peanut oil and wrap each half in waxed paper. Set the wrapped halves on a plate for easy handling and microwave on full power for about 5 minutes, turning the halves midway. Let them stand for 3 minutes.

Meanwhile, in a small bowl combine the vinegar, soy sauce, peanut butter, honey and oil, cover with vented plastic wrap and microwave on full power for about 20 seconds, then stir to combine. The idea here is to soften the peanut butter.

Slice the eggplant into chunks and toss them into a serving bowl with the peanut butter mixture. Sprinkle in the scallions and sesame seeds and toss to combine. Serve warm.

Rehydrating Dried Mushrooms

The most commonly available types are porcini and shiitake. Both are richly flavored and enhance no-salt-added recipes. To rehydrate in the microwave, remove the stems from four shiitake, rinse and toss into a large bowl to avoid boilovers. Pour in enough water to cover mushrooms, cover with vented plastic wrap and microwave on full power for about 5 minutes. Let stand for 5 minutes. Slice and add to omelettes or vegetable dishes or stuff whole. Use the flavorful cooking water in soups or sauces.

Dried porcini mushrooms don't have stems to remove and cooking time is about 4½ minutes.

What's Wakame?

A long-leafed sea vegetable that's available dry in packages at Oriental markets and many supermarkets. It tastes like kale, but it is sweeter. To microwave, rinse two 5-inch (12-cm) pieces in water to remove the natural salt on their surfaces. Then set them in a microwave-safe dish with about 1 cup (240 ml) of water, cover with vented plastic wrap and microwave on full power for 1½ minutes. Let stand for about a minute, drain and pat dry. You'll have about ⅔ cup (160 ml). Slice away the tough ribs, chop the tender leaves and toss them with greens or other vegetables or add to soups and stews the last minute of cooking. You can also serve the wakame leaves tossed with a splash each of sesame oil and soy sauce and toasted sesame seeds.

Microwaving Dried Tomatoes

Dried tomatoes are bold and rich in flavor. Just one taste and you will find them irresistible.

To microwave, set four dried tomatoes in a little bowl with enough chicken stock to cover. Cover the bowl with vented plastic wrap and microwave on full power for 1½ to 2 minutes, depending on size. Let them stand until they're cool enough to handle, then slice or mince and add to omelettes or toss with pasta or other vegetables. Use the newly flavored stock to cook other vegetables or add it to tomato or vegetable soups.

Dried tomatoes are available at specialty foods stores, Italian markets and many supermarkets. The best kind to buy are the unsalted ones.

BUTTERFLIED EGGPLANT WITH GARLIC AND OLIVE OIL

4 servings • 45 calories per serving

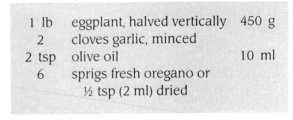

1 lb	eggplant, halved vertically	450 g
2	cloves garlic, minced	
2 tsp	olive oil	10 ml
6	sprigs fresh oregano or	
	½ tsp (2 ml) dried	

Rub the cut sides of the eggplant with the garlic and oil. Press in the sprigs, wrap each half in waxed paper and place cut side down on a plate. Microwave on full power for about 5 minutes, turning the halves midway. Let the halves stand for 5 minutes.

If your microwave has browning capability, brown the eggplant, cut side up, for about 5 minutes, or until it's a medium mottled brown. If not, run it under the broiler or grill for about 5 minutes. And if you do grill, oil the rack first to keep the eggplant from sticking. Slice and serve warm or room temperature with grilled chicken or lamb.

Garnishing with Eggs

Hard-cooked, chopped egg is a wonderful texture and color contrast to cooked vegetables like green beans, peas and spinach. To microwave a hard-cooked egg, first make sure it's room temperature. Then break it into a tiny dish or ramekin and puncture the yolk with a thin, sharp knife. This will keep it from exploding. Then cover with unvented plastic wrap and microwave on medium power for about 2 minutes. Let it stand until cool enough to handle, then chop over cooked vegetables.

This may not be the prettiest hard-cooked egg you've ever seen but when it's chopped nobody will ever know. If you're avoiding egg yolks, chop and use only the whites. The egg also makes a fast, delicious breakfast when topped with plain, low-fat yogurt and fresh dill.

Ears in the Husk

To microwave two ears of corn, strip off any ugly—loose or brown, for example—leaves, chop off the tassels and rinse well. Set the ears, still very wet, on a plate and microwave, uncovered, on full power about 5 minutes for sweet corn and 5½ to 6 minutes for yellow corn. Turn the ears a couple of times during cooking. Let stand until cool enough to handle, 3 to 4 minutes, then remove husks and serve.

Lower-Fat Herb Butter for Ears in the Husk

Makes enough for 2 ears • 82 calories per Tbs (15 ml)

2 tsp	sweet butter	10 ml
2 Tbs	chicken stock	30 ml
½ tsp	minced herb or herbs, like basil, thyme, tarragon, rosemary, or minced shallots	2 ml
½ tsp	Dijon-style mustard	2 ml

In a small bowl combine the butter, stock and herb or herbs. Cover with vented plastic wrap and microwave on full power for about 1 minute, or until the butter is melted. Whisk in the mustard and drizzle over ears or 1 lb (450 g) or warm vegetables.

Dealing with Redskins

It's best to use these waxy-type potatoes when microwaving because the starchy types (baking potatoes) can become gummy when microwaved. If you don't know which type you have, cut one in half and then rub the two halves together. If they stick, it's a starchy potato and shouldn't be microwaved.

To microwave redskins, start with 1 pound (450 g) of potatoes (about four) and chop into 1-inch (2.5-cm) chunks. Toss them into a 9-inch (23-cm) glass pie dish with ¼ cup (60 ml) of chicken stock and cover with vented plastic wrap. Microwave on full power for 6½ to 7 minutes, stirring or shaking a couple of times during cooking. Let them stand for about 4 minutes before draining and tossing with flavorings.

Ideas for Flavorings

- Freshly grated Parmesan and a pinch of oregano
- Pesto
- Plain, low-fat yogurt, minced purple onions and dillweed
- A handful of corn kernels, pinch of chili powder, minced sweet red peppers and a splash of olive oil
- Chopped ripe tomatoes, minced garlic, crushed rosemary and a splash of olive oil

WARM ZUCCHINI MOUSSE WITH TOMATO SAUCE AND MOZZARELLA

4 servings • 113 calories per serving

½ lb	zucchini, grated	225 g
2 Tbs	finely minced onions	30 ml
2	cloves garlic, finely minced	
½ tsp	sage	2 ml
¼ tsp	thyme	1 ml
pinch	cayenne pepper or other ground red pepper	
2	eggs	
¾ cup	milk	180 ml
	olive oil	
½ cup	tomato sauce	120 ml
¼ cup	grated mozzarella	60 ml

Scoop the zucchini into a small bowl. Cover with vented plastic wrap and microwave on full power for 2 minutes. Dump the zucchini into a strainer and press it to get rid of the liquid. Let it drain while you prepare the rest of the ingredients.

In a medium bowl combine the onions, garlic, sage, thyme, cayenne or other red pepper, eggs and milk. Mix well but gently, don't make bubbles. Add the zucchini and combine.

Lightly oil 4 microwave-safe ½-cup (120-ml) ramekins or custard cups with olive oil and pour an equal portion of the zucchini mixture into each. Set the ramekins on a plate for easy handling, then microwave, uncovered, on full power for about 4 minutes, rotating midway. Let stand for 2 minutes.

Meanwhile, divide the tomato sauce among 4 serving plates. Unmold a mousse onto each plate and immediately sprinkle with mozzarella. It's important to do this while the mousse is still warm so the mozzarella can melt.

BABY PATTYPANS WITH BALSAMIC VINAIGRETTE

If you can't locate baby pattypans, use adult pattypans cut into 1-inch (2.5-cm) squares. If you don't have roasted peppers on hand, canned pimientos will do.

4 servings • 61 calories per serving

1 lb	baby pattypan squash	450 g
1 Tbs	balsamic vinegar	15 ml
1 Tbs	cider vinegar	15 ml
1 Tbs	olive oil	15 ml
pinch	dry mustard	
2	roasted sweet red peppers, thinly sliced	
	freshly ground black pepper for sprinkling	

Rinse the pattypans and tip into a 9-inch (23-cm) glass pie dish while still wet. Cover with vented plastic wrap and microwave on full power for about 4½ minutes. Let stand for 3 minutes.

Meanwhile, in a small bowl combine the vinegars, oil, mustard and red peppers. Drain and add the squash, sprinkle with black pepper and toss to combine. Serve warm or chilled.

FROM RIVERS AND SEAS

The best part about microwaving fish is that the speed of cooking leaves it moist and succulent without lots of added fat and calories. I prefer to cook fish purchased fresh from the market. But if you must use frozen, defrost it in the refrigerator first. This will give you fish in prime form, and you won't need to hide inferior textures and flavors with fatty sauces.

One pound (450 g) of most fish will take 4 to 5 minutes to cook on full power in a 600- to 700-watt microwave. (If you have a 500-watt microwave, add 1 to 2 minutes to that time or check the Cooking Time Chart chart on page 8.) Now some people will write and say "My fish only took 2 minutes to cook" or "I cooked my fish for 15 minutes and it was still raw." And yes, the time will vary depending on whether you're microwaving whole fish, fillets or chunks. For example, tiny, delicate bay scallops will take much less time than a thick tuna steak, and whole fish will take longer than a fillet.

Also, fish will vary in size. For example, some bluefish come five to the pound (450 g) and some you can barely lift by yourself. In most recipes, varieties of fish can substitute for each other as long as they're of similar size and texture. You wouldn't use perch in a swordfish recipe, but you could use tuna. Here is a list of fish that are interchangeable for the recipes in this book:

Small Fillets	Medium Fillets	Large Fillets and Steaks	Small Whole Fish
Black Bass	Mackerel	Swordfish	Lake Trout
Tautaug	Red Snapper	Tuna	Whiting
Rock Bass	Grouper	Halibut	Perch
Small Ocean Perch	Haddock	Shark	Small Bluefish
Lake or Sea Trout	Catfish	Monkfish	Porgy
Sea Bass	Salmon Fillet	Large Bluefish	Croaker
Flounder	Orange Roughy	Tilefish	
Plaice	Salmon Trout	Mahi Mahi	
Sole	Medium Ocean	Salmon Steak	
Fluke	Perch	Grouper Steak	
	Amberjack	Marlin	
	Pompano	Kingfish	
	Medium Bluefish		
	Redfish		

More Fish Tips

Before cooking a fillet check to see that it's of even thickness. If not (and most fillets aren't), tuck the thinner ends under the middle so the whole fillet will cook evenly.

Try to avoid microwaving fish directly on paper towels because it can stick and be difficult to remove. Scallops are especially famous for this. Instead, set the fish directly on a plate or dish and drain before serving or saucing.

Peel shrimp before microwaving. I admit that the shells make cute little packages, but they tend to stick to the flesh and are often difficult to remove. If you don't want the peeled shrimp to curl during microwaving, skewer them with toothpicks.

SALMON TROUT WITH MUSTARD AND DILL

This is a tasty and beautiful river fish with pale coral flesh and silvery skin. If you can't find it, use salmon fillet instead. Either way, it's delicious served with redskin potatoes and mustard on the side.

4 servings • 164 calories per serving

2 tsp	Dijon-style mustard	10 ml
2 Tbs	rice vinegar	30 ml
¾ tsp	coriander seeds, finely crushed	3 ml
1 Tbs	chopped fresh dill	15 ml
5	black peppercorns, finely crushed	
1 lb	salmon trout fillet	450 g

In a 9-inch (23-cm) glass pie dish combine the mustard, vinegar, coriander, dill and peppercorns. Wipe the skin side of the salmon trout with the marinade, then set it skin side up in the dish and let it marinate for 2 hours in the refrigerator.

If the ends of the fish are thinner than the middle, tuck them under so the fish will cook evenly. Cover with vented plastic wrap and microwave on full power for about 5 minutes. Let stand for 3 minutes and remove the skin before serving warm or chilled.

Dill Butter

Fragrant and rich, it's hard to believe this is a recipe that's reduced in fat, calories and sodium. Serve it with poached fish and shellfish.

Makes about ¼ cup or enough for 1 lb of fish • 23 calories per Tbs

2 tsp	sweet butter	10 ml
1 Tbs	freshly squeezed lemon juice	15 ml
2 Tbs	freshly squeezed orange juice	30 ml
¼ tsp	dillweed	1 ml

Combine all of the ingredients in a small bowl, cover with vented plastic wrap and microwave on full power until the butter has melted, 40 to 60 seconds. Use warm or room temperature.

RED SNAPPER WITH JALAPEÑO BUTTER

The low-fat butter can be made ahead and refrigerated until you're ready.

4 servings • 144 calories per serving

2	jalapeño peppers, halved with seeds and pith removed (wear plastic gloves when handling)	
1	clove garlic	
1 tsp	sweet butter	5 ml
1 tsp	freshly squeezed lemon juice	5 ml
¼ cup	cottage cheese	60 ml
1	lemon, thinly sliced	
1 lb	red snapper fillets (4 pieces)	450 g

To prepare the butter, toss the jalapeño halves into a small dish with the garlic, butter and lemon juice. Cover with vented plastic wrap and microwave on full power for about 1 minute.

Then tip the mixture into a blender or processor and puree until smooth, adding the cottage cheese while the motor is running. Set aside or store, refrigerated, while you prepare the fish.

Set the lemon slices in a 9-inch (23-cm) glass pie dish. Arrange the fish skin side up on top of the lemon slices and cover with vented plastic wrap. Microwave on full power for about 4½ minutes, rotating the dish midway. Then let the fish stand for 4 minutes. Serve hot with skin removed and a knob of jalapeño butter on top of each fillet.

SHARK STEAK WITH FENNEL AIOLI

This is a good way to use a browning dish for cooking fish. If you don't have one, microwave the shark in a 9-inch (23-cm) glass pie dish, covered with vented plastic wrap, for about 4½ minutes, flipping midway.

1 lb	shark steak, about ¾-inch (2-cm) thick	450 g
	olive oil for brushing	
1 Tbs	olive oil	15 ml
3	cloves garlic	
½ tsp	fennel seeds	2 ml

4 servings • 191 calories per serving

Preheat a browning dish for about 4½ minutes, or according to the manufacturer's directions. When it's ready, work quickly to brush it with oil if it is not a nonstick dish. Set the shark on it and cover with crumpled waxed paper. Microwave on full power for 1 to 1½ minutes, flip and microwave for 1 to 1½ minutes more. Let the shark stand while you make the aioli.

In a small bowl combine the oil, garlic and fennel seeds. Cover tightly with vented plastic wrap and microwave on full power for 1½ to 2 minutes. Scoop the mixture into a mortar and crush into a paste. Rub the paste all over the shark and let it stand for a couple of minutes to infuse before serving.

Note: The crumpled waxed paper here is merely to keep the shark from splattering all over your microwave, so keep it loose. Food cooked on a browning dish should not be covered, or it will steam instead of sear.

SHRIMP FROM RIO

This exceptional combination of plump shrimp, hearts of palm, rice and saffron reminds me of an authentic dish prepared by my Brazilian friend, Dyla. By microwaving, you can cut calories and fat from the original concept.

4 servings • 231 calories per serving

1 lb	large shrimp, peeled	450 g
1½ cups	cooked rice	360 ml
¼ cup	minced green peppers	60 m
¼ cup	minced sweet red peppers	60 ml
⅓ cup	finely minced onions	80 ml
5	hearts of palm, sliced into disks	
½ tsp	oregano	2 ml
¼ tsp	saffron, crumbled	1 ml
2 Tbs	freshly squeezed orange juice	30 ml
¼ cup	chicken stock	60 ml
2 Tbs	freshly grated Parmesan	30 ml

Rinse the shrimp and set it, still wet, around the rim of a large, flat plate, and if you don't want them to curl, skewer each with a toothpick. Cover the plate with vented plastic wrap and microwave on full power for 3 to 4 minutes. Let the shrimp stand for 4 minutes.

Meanwhile, in a 1-quart (1-liter) dish, combine the rice, peppers, onions, hearts of palm, oregano, saffron, orange juice and stock. Cover and microwave on full power for about 3 minutes, stirring midway. Add the shrimp and Parmesan and mix until the rice is colored by the saffron. Let stand for a couple of minutes before serving to allow the flavors to become acquainted.

SCALLOPS WITH DRIED TOMATOES

Ensure even cooking by using scallops that are all about the same size.

4 servings • 219 calories per serving

4	dried tomatoes	
1	clove garlic	
1	shallot	
⅓ cup	chicken stock	80 ml
1	bay leaf	
¼ cup	chicken stock	60 ml
1 Tbs	olive oil	15 ml
pinch	thyme	pinch
1 Tbs	freshly grated Parmesan	15 ml
1 lb	sea scallops	450 g
	lemon juice for sprinkling	

In a small bowl combine the dried tomatoes, garlic, shallot, ⅓ cup (80 ml) of stock and bay leaf. Cover with vented plastic wrap and microwave on full power for about 3 minutes. Remove the bay leaf and scoop the mixture into a processor or blender and whiz until combined and smooth. With the motor running add in the ¼ cup (60 ml) of stock, oil, thyme and Parmesan. Let the sauce stand while you prepare the scallops.

Arrange the scallops in a ring around the rim of a large, round plate and sprinkle with lemon juice. Cover with crumpled waxed paper and microwave on full power for 4 to 4½ minutes, rotating the plate midway. Let the scallops stand for about 2 minutes, remove them from the liquid they're sitting in and toss with the sauce and serve.

Note: Avoid microwaving scallops on paper towels because they tend to stick and can be difficult to remove. One fun way is to set about a pound (450 g) in a bamboo steamer that's been lined with waxed paper so they won't fall through. Set the steamer on a plate, cover and microwave on full power for 4 to 4½ minutes, rotating midway.

Perfect Fish in Parchment Paper

This is a drier vehicle for cooking than the tightly covered glass and plastic dishes you may be used to. It's great for recipes where you don't want to use a lot of liquid and for fish that are naturally moist or still have their skin. Bass, trout, flounder and sole are examples of fish that microwave well in parchment paper.

The method is simple. To begin you'll need a 20-inch (50-cm) piece of household parchment paper, which is enough to microwave 1 pound (450 g) of fish. Set the fish (skin side down if it's got it) on one half of the paper. Next, rub the flesh of the fish with spices, herbs, mustard or other aromatics and sprinkle with sliced vegetables. Then fold the paper over and crimp the edges closed. Unlike conventional cooking, you don't need to rub the paper with oil. Set the package on a plate for easy handling and microwave on full power for about 4½ minutes. Let stand for 4 minutes. When you open the package, stand back or you could get a faceful of steam. Depending on the ingredients you choose for your package, there may be some liquid at the bottom, which can be avoided by carefully lifting the fish onto a serving plate.

For fun, prepare each serving in an individual package, and let each diner open his or her own. Or, instead of parchment paper, use a large, brown paper bag. Set it on a plate for support, set the ingredients inside, then fold the bag and tuck the top part under to seal. Cook on full power for about 4½ minutes per pound (450 g) of fish, the same as for parchment.

Pickled Ginger

Known best as the pungent accompaniment to Japanese *sashimi,* pickled ginger is also exceptional with cold poached fish. To prepare, combine 2 tablespoons (30 ml) very finely minced fresh ginger, 1 tablespoon (15 ml) rice vinegar, ½ teaspoon (2 ml) honey and a pinch of ground ginger in a small bowl. Cover with vented plastic wrap and microwave on full power for 1½ minutes. Chill before serving and store in the refrigerator up to one week.

BLACK BASS IN PARCHMENT

If you can't find black bass, use trout fillets instead.

4 servings • 156 calories per serving

Lay the fish, skin side down, on one half of a 20-inch (50-cm) piece of household parchment paper. In a small bowl combine the chilies, red peppers, coriander, garlic, tomato juice, vinegar, oil and oregano and divide the mixture evenly over the tops of the fillets. Be sure all exposed flesh has been covered. Fold the paper over, crimp the edges closed and set the package on a plate for easy handling. Microwave on full power for about 4½ minutes, rotating the plate midway. Let stand for 4 minutes, then serve hot.

1 lb	black bass fillets (4 pieces)	450 g
1	mild green chili pepper, minced	
1	fresh hot chili pepper, like jalapeño, minced (wear plastic gloves when handling)	
1	sweet red pepper, cut into fine julienne	
2 Tbs	finely minced fresh coriander	30 ml
1	clove garlic, finely minced	
2 Tbs	tomato juice	30 ml
1 tsp	red wine vinegar	5 ml
1 tsp	olive oil	5 ml
½ tsp	oregano	2 ml

More Ideas for Flavorings

- Minced green olives, minced celery, bâtons of carrots and leeks and a splash of champagne vinegar
- Sliced purple onions, chopped leeks, almond slivers, saffron and orange juice
- Slivered sweet potatoes, minced scallions and Dijon-style mustard

SEA SALAD
WITH LEMON
AND WATERCRESS

This reminds me of seviche because, although the shellfish is cooked, it is plump, moist and surrounded by crisp flavors.

4 servings • 255 calories per serving

½ lb	sea scallops	225 g
	lemon juice for sprinkling	
½ lb	large shrimp, peeled	225 g
2 Tbs	freshly squeezed lemon juice	30 ml
2 tsp	olive oil	10 ml
¾ tsp	Dijon-style mustard	3 ml
2 Tbs	minced green olives	30 ml
	freshly ground black pepper to taste	
2 cups	watercress leaves	480 ml

Prepare the scallops by arranging them in a ring around the rim of a round plate. Sprinkle with lemon juice, cover with crumpled waxed paper and microwave on full power for 2 to 2½ minutes, rotating the plate midway. Let scallops stand while you prepare the remaining ingredients.

Arrange the shrimp in a ring around the rim of a round plate and skewer them with toothpicks if you don't want them to curl. Cover with crumpled waxed paper and microwave on full power for about 2 minutes, rotating the plate midway. Let the shrimp stand for 2 minutes, then toss them into a large serving bowl with the scallops.

Meanwhile, prepare the dressing in a small bowl by combining the lemon juice, oil, mustard, olives and black pepper. Pour over the scallops and shrimp. If you're serving immediately, toss in the watercress, if not, refrigerate and add the watercress when you're ready.

Note: Bay scallops can be substituted for the sea scallops and can be microwaved the same way. They'll cook much faster, though, so start checking for doneness at about 30 seconds.

SHRIMP WITH TWO FRAGRANT SAUCES

I know what you may have heard in the past about good results when microwaving shrimp in their shells, but forget it. Shrimp should be peeled before microwaving. When they're not, the shells can be difficult to remove; they stick to the flesh.

4 servings • 146 calories per serving

1 lb	jumbo shrimp (about 12), peeled	450 g
Dark and Fragrant Sauce		
1 Tbs	light soy sauce	15 ml
3 Tbs	chicken stock	45 ml
1 Tbs	*mirin**	15 ml
1 Tbs	finely minced fresh chives	15 ml
¼ tsp	minced fresh ginger	1 ml
splash	sesame oil	
splash	chili oil	
Fragrant Orange and Ginger Sauce		
1	orange, peeled and seeded	
½ tsp	minced fresh ginger	2 ml
1 tsp	honey	5 ml
1 tsp	rice vinegar	5 ml
2 Tbs	chicken stock	30 ml

To prepare the shrimp, line the bottom of your microwave with waxed paper and arrange the shrimp in a ring on top. Cover with crumpled waxed paper and microwave on full power for about 4 minutes, flipping the shrimp midway. Let them stand while you prepare the sauces.

For Dark and Fragrant Sauce, combine the soy sauce, stock, *mirin,* chives, ginger and oils in a small bowl and cover with vented plastic wrap. Microwave on full power for about 1 minute. Makes about ¼ cup (60 ml).

For Fragrant Orange and Ginger Sauce, combine the oranges, ginger, honey, vinegar and stock in a processor or blender

and whiz until combined. Pour the sauce into a small bowl, cover with vented plastic wrap and microwave on full power for about 1 minute. Makes about ½ cup (120 ml).

When you're ready to serve, arrange the shrimp on a serving plate along with the two fragrant sauces.

*Available at Oriental markets.

(continued)

Notes:

- You can use smaller shrimp, but remember that they'll take less time to microwave, so watch them.
- The Dark and Fragrant Sauce is delicious with mild white fish, scallops and poached chicken. Try the Fragrant Orange and Ginger Sauce with crab legs or soft-shelled crabs.

MUSSELS WITH TOMATOES AND FRESH BASIL

To ensure even cooking, the mussels are microwaved in three batches. Serve as a light lunch or dinner with Parmesan for sprinkling, fresh greens and crusty bread.

4 servings • 93 calories per serving

⅓ cup	fresh basil leaves	80 ml
2	cloves garlic, minced	
8	plum tomatoes	
1 Tbs	red wine vinegar	15 ml
36	mussels, cleaned and beards removed	

Combine the basil, garlic, tomatoes and vinegar in a processor or blender and whiz until combined and smooth. Pour a third of the tomato mixture into a 9-inch (23-cm) glass pie dish and add in a third of the mussels. Cover with vented plastic wrap and microwave on full power until the mussels are open, about 2 minutes.

Then dump the mussels and sauce into a huge serving bowl and cover with foil, to keep them warm, while you microwave the remaining batches. Let the mussels stand for several minutes before serving to give the flavors time to become acquainted. Be sure to dip each mussel into the sauce before enjoying.

CLAMS WITH CUCUMBER-LEEK SAUCE

This is a tasty, low-calorie, low-salt alternative to clams dunked in butter.

4 servings • 138 calories per serving

2	leeks	
½ cup	chicken stock	120 ml
1	bay leaf	
1	cucumber, peeled, seeded and chopped	
½ tsp	dillweed	2 ml
½ tsp	summer savory	2 ml
2 Tbs	buttermilk	30 ml
1 tsp	Dijon-style mustard	5 ml
¼ tsp	freshly grated lemon peel	1 ml
48	little neck clams, rinsed and scrubbed	

Trim the leeks of their roots and tough green parts, then chop. Scoop into a strainer and rinse out the sand and grit. When they're clean, dump them into a medium bowl with the stock and bay leaf, cover and microwave on full power for about 4 minutes, stirring or shaking midway. Add the cucumbers and continue to microwave for 2 minutes more.

Remove bay leaf and scoop the mixture right into a processor or blender, add the dillweed, savory, buttermilk, mustard and lemon and whiz until smooth. Let the sauce relax in the refrigerator for about an hour.

When you're ready, set as many clams as will fit in a ring along the rim of a large, round plate with the part that opens facing the center. Cover with crumpled waxed paper and microwave on full power until the clams open, which should begin at about 2½ minutes. You may remove the clams as they open to avoid overcooking. They should all be open at about 5½ minutes, and those that aren't should be discarded. Reserve the liquid at the bottom of the plate and repeat with remaining clams until all have cooked.

To serve, arrange the clams on half shells on a serving platter with a spoonful of cucumber-leek sauce atop each.

(continued)

Notes:

- You'll have about ¼ cup (60 ml) of liquid, or clam stock, from each dozen clams. Strain it through fine cheesecloth or paper towels to remove grit, then use it in fish soups, fish sauces or warm tomato soup.

- You'll have about 1⅓ cups (320 ml) of cucumber-leek sauce, which is more than you need for the clams. It keeps, refrigerated, for about a week and can be enjoyed with poached salmon, poached chicken or mussels.

POACHED FRESH TUNA WITH AROMATICS

This is a nice example of how the right balance of flavorings can be a satisfying substitute for salt. If you can't find fresh marjoram, substitute fresh basil or fresh coriander.

4 servings • 168 calories per serving

1 Tbs	minced fresh marjoram	15 ml
¾ tsp	minced fresh ginger	3 ml
3 Tbs	freshly squeezed orange juice	45 ml
1 lb	tuna steaks (2 pieces)	450 g

In a 9-inch (23-cm) glass pie dish combine the marjoram, ginger and orange juice. If necessary, slice away and discard any dark parts from the tuna, then add it to the marinade, making sure both sides are coated. Let marinate for about 2 hours in the refrigerator, flipping midway.

Cover the dish with vented plastic wrap and microwave on full power for 4 to 4½ minutes, rotating the dish midway. Let stand for about 3 minutes and serve hot.

HADDOCK WITH CHILI PASTE AND SWEET PEPPER SLIVERS

This reminds me of an African recipe called **Moqueca** *(Mo-KEE-sah), except the original is far higher in fat and, of course, not microwaved.*

4 servings • 131 calories per serving

½ tsp	coriander seeds	2 ml
¼ cup	chopped sweet onions	60 ml
3	cloves garlic	
1	small hot chili pepper	
	juice of 1 lime	
1 Tbs	tomato paste	15 ml
1 tsp	peanut oil	5 ml
1 lb	haddock fillet	450 g
	peanut oil for painting, if necessary	
1	sweet red pepper, slivered finely minced fresh parsley for sprinkling	

In a mortar or spice grinder, mash the coriander seeds, onions, garlic, chili, lime juice, tomato paste and oil into a smooth paste. Rub the paste on the haddock and let it marinate for about an hour in the refrigerator.

Preheat a browning dish for 4½ minutes or according to manufacturer's instructions. When it's ready, paint the dish with a bit of oil, if it is not a nonstick dish, and quickly set the haddock on it. Cover with crumpled waxed paper to prevent splattering and microwave on full power for 1 to 1½ minutes, then flip the haddock over and toss the pepper slivers on top. Replace the waxed paper and microwave for 1 to 1½ minutes more. Let the haddock stand for a couple of minutes before sprinkling with parsley and serving.

SOFT SHELLS WITH WARM MUSTARD SAUCE

This is a great way to enjoy soft-shelled crab without sautéing in butter and oil.

4 servings • 225 calories per serving

8	soft-shelled crabs, cleaned	
8	bay leaves	
Warm Mustard Sauce		
¼ cup	buttermilk	60 ml
1 tsp	Dijon-style mustard	5 ml
1 tsp	coarse prepared mustard	5 ml
pinch	dry mustard	

Microwave the soft shells 4 at a time, by setting them, evenly spaced, around the rim of a round plate. Tuck a bay leaf under each, cover with crumpled waxed paper and microwave on full power for 4½ to 5 minutes, flipping them over midway. Repeat with the remaining crabs and let them stand while you prepare the sauce.

For the Warm Mustard Sauce, combine the buttermilk and mustards in a small dish and cover with vented plastic wrap. Microwave on full power for 20 to 25 seconds. If the sauce breaks it's because of the vinegar in the mustards. It easily stirs back into a smooth sauce for serving.

Notes:

- To microwave king crab legs, set 4 legs (8 oz or 225 g each) into a bamboo steamer. Sprinkle with lemon juice and stick a lemon slice on the exposed snowy white flesh of the shoulder. Cover the steamer and set it on a plate to catch the drips. Microwave on full power for 7 to 8 minutes, rotating the legs midway. Let them stand for about 3 minutes before serving. This will serve 4 as part of a light lunch or dinner and is great with Warm Mustard Sauce.

- Crab claws can be prepared in the same manner as king crab legs. Arrange them in a ring around the edge of the bamboo steamer with the parts that pinch facing in. Sixteen claws will take 3 to 3½ minutes on full power.

ORANGE ROUGHY WITH TOMATO, LEMON AND MINT

Whether this Australian fish deserves its name or not, it sure looks like the thug of the sea. In contrast, its flesh is clean and tasty. If you can't find it, use flounder instead.

4 servings • 182 calories per serving

1	ripe tomato, sliced	
2	cloves garlic, finely minced	
1 lb	orange roughy fillets	450 g
1 Tbs	finely minced fresh mint	15 ml
1	lemon, thinly sliced	
½ tsp	oregano	2 ml
⅓ cup	crumbled feta cheese	80 ml

The idea here is to build this dish in layers with the fish in the middle of everything. Start with a 9-inch (23-cm) glass pie dish and arrange the tomato slices in the bottom. Sprinkle the garlic over the tomatoes and arrange the fish over it. Next, sprinkle in the mint, layer on the lemon slices and finally, sprinkle with the oregano. Let the whole thing sit for about 30 minutes.

When ready, cover with vented plastic wrap and microwave on full power for 4½ to 5 minutes. Let it stand for 5 minutes. To serve, lift the fish and tomatoes onto a serving platter. Sprinkle with the feta and serve hot.

Chopped Spinach for Stuffing

Instead of using frozen spinach, try fresh. It takes less time and it's more healthful because its nutrients haven't been processed away. Start with 2 cups (480 ml) of packed leaves and mince them in a processor. Then toss them into a 9-inch (23-cm) glass pie dish, cover with vented plastic wrap and microwave on full power for about 1 minute. Let stand for 1 minute, then drain. You'll have about ⅓ cup (80 ml) and you can use it in stuffings for flounder fillets, whole fish or boneless breasts of chicken.

SEAFOOD SAUSAGE WITH AVOCADO CREAM

Light years away from the fat-laden sausages many people are used to.

4 servings • 290 calories per serving

½ lb	salmon fillet	225 g
½ lb	bluefish fillet	225 g
1 cup	cooked rice	240 ml
pinch	cayenne pepper or other ground red pepper	
¼ tsp	freshly grated lemon peel	1 ml
2 Tbs	lemon juice	30 ml
¼ cup	minced carrots	60 ml
¼ cup	minced onions	60 ml
¼ cup	minced celery	60 ml
1	shallot, finely minced	
1	ripe avocado	
2 Tbs	buttermilk	30 ml
1	clove garlic, finely minced	
pinch	freshly grated lemon peel	

To prepare the sausage, combine the salmon, bluefish, rice, cayenne or other red pepper, lemon peel and juice, carrots, onions, celery and shallots in a processor and whiz until smooth, but keep the tiny vegetable pieces distinguishable. Shape the mixture into 4 sausage shapes, about 5 × 1½ inches (12 × 4 cm) and wrap each tightly in a square of plastic wrap. Set the sausages evenly spaced around the rim of a round plate and microwave on full power for about 4½ minutes, rotating the plate midway. Set the sausages, plate and all, in the refrigerator and let them chill overnight so the flavors can mingle.

When you're ready, prepare the avocado cream by combining the avocado, buttermilk, garlic and lemon peel in a processor. Whiz until combined.

The sausages can be served chilled, straight from the refrigerator, or if your microwave has a browning unit you can glaze them for 2 to 3 minutes on each side. You can also glaze the sausages under a conventional broiler.

LOUISIANA CATFISH WITH YA-YA RICE

Scrod or haddock are good substitutes for the catfish. And don't let the long ingredient list scare you away. The whole recipe only takes two steps.

4 servings • 185 calories per serving

Set the catfish in a 9-inch (23-cm) glass pie dish and tuck the bay leaves underneath. Cover with vented plastic wrap and microwave on full power for 2 to 2½ minutes, rotating the dish midway. Let the catfish stand while you prepare the rice.

In a medium bowl, combine the rice, onions, peppers, tomatoes, celery, garlic, chilies, chili powder, cumin, Worcestershire, hot pepper sauce, mustard and oregano. Cover and microwave on full power for about 3 minutes, stirring or shaking midway. Crumble the catfish into the rice and add the butter and scallions, mixing well to combine. Let the whole thing stand for 1 to 2 minutes, then serve.

½ lb	catfish fillet	225 g
3	bay leaves	
2 cups	cooked rice	480 ml
⅓ cup	minced onions	80 ml
¼ cup	minced green peppers	60 ml
¼ cup	minced sweet red peppers	60 ml
2	tomatoes, peeled, seeded and chopped	
¼ cup	minced celery, leaves too	60 ml
3	cloves garlic, minced	
1	hot chili pepper, seeded and minced	
½ tsp	Mexican-type chili powder	2 ml
½ tsp	cumin seeds, ground	2 ml
2 tsp	Worcestershire sauce	10 ml
¼ tsp	hot pepper sauce	1 ml
pinch	dry mustard	
½ tsp	oregano	2 ml
2 tsp	sweet butter	10 ml
2	scallions, minced	

TUNA STEAK
WITH GREEN PEPPER
PUREE

Red or yellow peppers may be substituted for the green.

4 servings • 214 calories per serving

In a 9-inch (23-cm) glass pie dish combine the vinegar, oil, chilies and mustard seeds. Add the tuna and baste it with the marinade. Tuck the chilies under the tuna and let it marinate for about 30 minutes in the refrigerator, turning midway.

Meanwhile, drop the peppers into a large dish. Add the onions to the peppers along with the garlic and stock. Cover and microwave on full power for about 5 minutes, stirring or shaking midway. Then let it stand while you prepare the tuna.

Cover the tuna with vented plastic wrap and microwave on full power for about 4½ minutes, flipping it over midway. Let the tuna stand for about 4 minutes.

Meanwhile, finish the pepper puree. Drain off the liquid and then pour the mixture into a processor or blender and whiz until combined and smooth. Discard the marinade and serve the tuna in puddles of puree.

3 Tbs	cider vinegar	45 ml
splash	olive oil	
2	dried hot chili peppers	
½ tsp	mustard seeds	2 ml
1 lb	tuna steak	450 g
3	green peppers, seeded, cored and chopped	
1	medium onion, quartered	
1	clove garlic, minced	
1 cup	beef stock	240 ml

Pungent Paprika

Traditionally, paprika is sautéed in butter or oil to release its aroma and flavor. By microwaving, you can completely omit the fat. Pour ½ teaspoon (2 ml) of paprika into a small dish and cover with vented plastic wrap. Microwave on full power for 1 minute, stopping twice to shake the dish. The paprika, now more aromatic and colorful, can be sprinkled on poached fish or added to pale sauces.

HOT AND SOUR SHRIMP WITH CRUNCHY LETTUCE

Normally I ignore iceberg lettuce, but in this recipe it provides a certain crunch and has the ability to absorb surrounding flavors.

4 servings • 195 calories per serving

Arrange the shrimp around the rim of a large, round plate. If you don't want them to curl, skewer them with toothpicks. Cover with crumpled waxed paper and microwave on full power for about 4 minutes, flipping the shrimp over midway. Let them stand while you prepare the sauce.

In a medium dish combine the cornstarch, ¼ cup (60 ml) stock and the mushrooms. Cover and microwave on full power until it thickens, about 1 minute. Whisk to combine, then add the scallions, tofu, garlic, hot pepper sauce, soy sauce, ½ cup stock and vinegar, cover and microwave on full power for 30 seconds. Stir in the oil and shrimp and let the mixture stand for about 2 minutes. Serve hot over the shredded lettuce.

1 lb	large shrimp, peeled	450 g
1 Tbs	cornstarch	15 ml
¼ cup	chicken stock	60 ml
3	dried shiitake mushrooms, chopped	
2	scallions, minced	
¼ cup	tofu, minced	60 ml
2	cloves garlic, minced	
7	drops hot pepper sauce, or to taste	
1 tsp	light soy sauce	5 ml
½ cup	chicken stock	120 ml
2 Tbs	cider vinegar	30 ml
1 tsp	toasted sesame oil	5 ml
2 cups	shredded iceberg lettuce	480 ml

Unfried Garlic

Many conventional fish recipes require you to sauté garlic in butter or oil, but you can conserve on fat and calories by microwaving instead. Simply combine four cloves of garlic, chopped, in a small bowl with 2 tablespoons (30 ml) of chicken stock. Cover with vented plastic wrap and microwave on full power for about 2 minutes, stirring or shaking midway. Then use as you would sautéed garlic.

East Indian Barbecue Seasoning (*Tikka* Paste)

This seasoning, known as tikka *paste, is usually made of spices, pureed fruit and lots of oil. Here, most of the fat is omitted and the flavors have been rearranged to create a delicious and fragrant sauce for shrimp, flounder, or other mild fish fillets.*

Makes about ⅔ cup or enough for 1 lb of fish • 123 calories per recipe

½ tsp	Mexican-type chili powder	2 ml
¼ tsp	turmeric	1 ml
pinch	ground cinnamon	
pinch	curry powder	
2	cloves garlic, smashed	
2 Tbs	chopped onions	30 ml
½ cup	chopped pineapple	120 ml
¼ cup	apple juice	60 ml
1 tsp	sweet butter	5 ml
1 tsp	cider vinegar	5 ml

In a medium bowl combine the chili powder, turmeric, cinnamon, curry powder, garlic, onions, pineapple and apple juice. Cover and microwave on full power for 2½ to 3 minutes, stirring or shaking midway. Scoop the mixture into a processor or blender and whiz until well combined and smooth, adding the butter and vinegar while the motor is running. Serve warm.

"In the Pink" Marinade

To create a pungent, low-calorie marinade for fish, combine ten pink peppercorns in a small dish with 2 tablespoons (30 ml) of raspberry vinegar. Cover with vented plastic wrap and microwave on full power for 1½ minutes. Then pour into a mortar and completely crush the peppercorns. Use to marinate 1 pound (450 g) of fish or veal.

Fish in an Oven Bag

These special cooking bags are available at most supermarkets, usually in the aluminum foil/waxed paper section. They're great for microwaving fish that appreciate extra-moist cooking, like swordfish, tuna steak, shark and small, whole fish like trout.

First shake about 1 tablespoon (15 ml) of flour around in the bag, then add about 1 pound (450 g) of fish. Then add about 1 cup (240 ml) of chopped fresh vegetables and herbs of your choice. Tomatoes, onions, basil and thyme is one combination that goes well with swordfish. Next, tie a knot in the top of the bag (*Do not* use the tie that comes with the bag, no matter what you've heard) and poke six or seven slits in the bag. Set it on a plate for easy handling and microwave on full power for about 4½ minutes, rotating the bag midway. Let stand for about 4 minutes before cutting the bag open to serve. Don't forget to use the no-fat-added sauce automatically created in the bottom of the bag.

CHILLED HADDOCK WITH SNOW PEAS AND ORANGE VINAIGRETTE

The haddock must be refrigerated overnight, so plan ahead.

4 servings • 166 calories per serving

1 lb	haddock fillet	450 g
1 cup	freshly squeezed orange juice	240 ml
1 tsp	orange juice concentrate	5 ml
1 tsp	Dijon-style mustard	5 ml
2 Tbs	cider vinegar	30 ml
1 Tbs	minced fresh parsley	15 ml
2 tsp	olive oil	10 ml
¼ cup	chicken stock	60 ml
¼ tsp	freshly grated orange peel	1 ml
¼ lb	Snow peas, strung if necessary	110 g

Set the haddock flat out in a 9-inch (23-cm) glass pie dish and pour the orange juice over it. Cover with vented plastic wrap and microwave on full power for about 4½ minutes. Let the haddock stand while you prepare the vinaigrette.

In a processor or blender combine the concentrate, mustard, vinegar, parsley, oil, stock and orange peel and whiz until smooth and combined. Pour the vinaigrette over the haddock (undrained), cover and refrigerate overnight.

When you're ready to serve, rinse the green beans and tip them into a medium bowl while still wet. Cover and microwave on full power for 45 to 60 seconds, depending on their size. Arrange the chilled haddock and vinaigrette on a serving plate with the beans alongside.

FLOUNDER MOSAICS

These disks of fish filled with colorful vegetables are far easier to prepare than your guests suspect.

4 servings • 126 calories per serving

1 Tbs	freshly squeezed lemon juice	15 ml
1 tsp	Dijon-style mustard	5 ml
½ tsp	thyme	2 ml
1 lb	flounder fillets (4 pieces)	450 g
1	small, sweet red pepper, cut into fine julienne	
1	small green pepper, cut into fine julienne	
1	small carrot, cut into fine julienne	

In a small bowl combine the lemon juice, mustard and thyme. Lay the fillets out flat and rub the juice mixture onto the sides that are facing up. Then set about 9 pieces of julienne vegetables across the narrow end of each fillet and roll to form bundles. Wrap each bundle in a square of plastic wrap.

Arrange the bundles evenly around the rim of a large plate and microwave on full power for about 4½ minutes, rotating and flipping the bundles over midway.

Let them stand until the bundles can easily be unwrapped, about 10 minutes. Use a sharp knife to slice each bundle into 1-inch (2.5-cm) disks. Serve hot or chilled.

Note: If you have extra julienne vegetables, finely mince them and use as a garnish.

Microwaving Rock Shrimp

Despite their tough exterior, rock shrimp are tender and delicious, especially when microwaved. They're tiny, about the size of two or three bay scallops, and they have a crisp flavor and texture. To prepare, first shell 1 pound (450 g) of shrimp and sprinkle with a bit of lemon juice or dry white wine. Arrange them in a ring around the rim of a large, round plate, cover with crumpled waxed paper and microwave on full power for about 3½ minutes, rotating the plate midway. Use them in shrimp or scallop recipes or toss with freshly cooked green beans and freshly grated Romano cheese.

SHRIMP IN A BAMBOO STEAMER

This is an interesting way to prepare fish. The steamer acts as a cooking container and can also be used as a serving dish for casual meals. If you microwave small pieces of fish or scallops, skewer them or line the steamer with a sheet of waxed paper so they won't fall through.

4 servings • 153 calories per serving

1 lb	jumbo shrimp, peeled and deveined	450 g
1 Tbs	freshly squeezed lemon juice	15 ml
1 Tbs	freshly squeezed orange juice	15 ml
1 tsp	olive oil	5 ml
pinch	freshly grated nutmeg	
1 Tbs	minced fresh basil	15 ml
1	clove garlic, minced	
	freshly ground black pepper to taste	
2	tangerines or oranges, seeded with pith removed	

In a medium bowl combine the shrimp, juices, oil, nutmeg, basil, garlic and pepper and let marinate for about an hour.

When you're ready, thread the shrimp and tangerine or orange sections on bamboo skewers and set them around the edge of the steamer. Set the steamer over a plate to catch drips and pour the remaining marinade over the skewers. Cover and microwave on full power for 4 to 4½ minutes, flipping the skewers over midway.

If you have a browning unit on your microwave, use it to glaze the skewers before serving. You can also run them under a conventional broiler until glazed. Glazing is not necessary, but if you decide to do it, first baste the skewers with Lemon-Orange Butter.

LEMON-ORANGE BUTTER

2 tsp	freshly squeezed lemon juice	10 ml
2 tsp	freshly squeezed orange juice	10 ml
1 tsp	sweet butter	5 ml

Combine all ingredients in a small bowl and cover with vented plastic wrap. Microwave on full power for about 1 minute, then use to baste shrimp or other fish.

FROG LEG SALAD WITH WHITE BEANS AND TINY PASTA

If you've only had frog legs when they've been deep-fried, try this light entrée. Serve with romaine and sprigs of watercress.

4 servings • 283 calories per serving

1½ lb	frog legs	675 g
1 Tbs	freshly squeezed lemon juice	15 ml
1	sweet red pepper, minced	
1	green pepper, minced	
2	scallions, minced	
1	shallot, minced	
2 Tbs	minced fresh parsley	30 ml
2 Tbs	minced fresh basil	30 ml
1 Tbs	grated provolone	15 ml
1 cup	cooked small white beans	240 ml
1 cup	cooked tiny pasta, like orzo, acini di pepe or ditalini	240 ml
3 Tbs	freshly squeezed lemon juice	45 ml
1 Tbs	safflower oil	15 ml
	freshly ground black pepper for sprinkling	

Arrange the frog legs in a starburst pattern on a large, round plate with the meaty parts on the outside. Sprinkle with the lemon juice and cover with vented plastic wrap. Microwave on full power for about 5½ minutes, flipping the legs over midway. Let them stand for 5 minutes while you prepare the rest of the salad.

In a large bowl combine the peppers, scallions, shallots, parsley, basil, provolone, beans, pasta, lemon juice and oil. When the legs are cool enough to handle, remove the meat, discarding the bones and black tendons. Shred the meat with your hands and add it to the rest of the salad, combining well. Sprinkle with freshly ground black pepper and serve room temperature or chilled.

WHOLE FISH WITH A FRAGRANT BOUQUET

1	scallion, minced		
2	cloves garlic, minced		
¼ tsp	minced fresh ginger	1 ml
4	small trout		
3 Tbs	freshly squeezed lime juice	45 ml
1 Tbs	minced fresh chives	15 ml

Small fish, about four to the pound (450 g), microwave more evenly than large whole fish. Use gutted small trout, whiting, croakers, porgy, tiny bluefish or whatever small fish is available fresh in your area.

4 servings • 107 calories per serving

Tuck the scallions, garlic and ginger into the cavities of the trout. Then rub the skins with the lime juice and chives. Wrap each trout in a square of plastic wrap and arrange evenly around the rim of a large plate. Microwave for about 5 minutes, flipping over midway.

Let the wrapped trout marinate overnight in the refrigerator. Serve chilled with a garlicky vinaigrette, prepared horseradish or Pickled Ginger (page 117).

More Ideas for Fragrant Bouquets

Fill the cavities of whole fish with:

- Fresh purple basil leaves
- Fennel stalks
- Finely minced celery, sweet onions and carrots
- Fresh rosemary sprigs

Ideas for Using Hoisin Sauce

Once you experience the pungency of this condiment, you'll invent many new ways to use it. Traditionally, it was used as a fish sauce in Chinese cooking. Now it is also used to enhance pork and poultry. Many westerners call it Chinese barbecue sauce and use it that way.

Hoisin is made of pureed red beans and spices and is available at Oriental markets and many supermarkets. To prepare the sauce for use, combine 2 tablespoons (30 ml) of hoisin sauce with 2 tablespoons (30 ml) of Chinese red vinegar or red wine vinegar in a small bowl. Cover with vented plastic wrap and microwave on full power until heated through, about 40 seconds. Use as a marinade for mild white fish like haddock, or hot or cold as a dipping sauce for cooked shrimp or crab.

SWORDFISH BROCHETTES WITH GREEN OLIVE MARINADE

If you like, you may rinse the olives in vinegar to free them of extra processing salt before using.

4 servings • 185 calories per serving

5	pitted green olives	
1	clove garlic	
1 tsp	prepared coarse mustard	5 ml
1 Tbs	freshly squeezed lemon juice	15 ml
2 Tbs	chicken stock	30 ml
1 tsp	olive oil	5 ml
1 Tbs	minced fresh parsley	15 ml
1 lb	swordfish, cut into 1-inch (2.5-cm) chunks	450 g
10 to 15	pitted black olives	
10 to 15	pitted green olives	

In a processor or blender combine the 5 small green olives, garlic, mustard, lemon juice, stock, oil and parsley and whiz until well combined and smooth. Scoop into a bowl with the swordfish chunks and let marinate for about 3 hours, stirring midway.

When you're ready to serve, thread the chunks on bamboo skewers, interspersed with the pitted black and green olives. Arrange the brochettes evenly around the rim of a large plate and pour any remaining marinade over them. Cover with crumpled waxed paper and micro-wave on full power for about 4 minutes, rearranging the brochettes midway.

If your microwave has a browning unit, you can use it to glaze the brochettes before serving. You can also run them under a conventional broiler for about a minute on each side.

BIRDS OF A
FEATHER

A recent culinary adventure gave me the opportunity to outfit a kitchen for 12 business people visiting from China. I arranged for an inspiring setup including ovens, stovetops, steamers and woks. Just for fun, I added a microwave.

Eventually the Chinese crew invited me to be their guest at a meal. I was excited to fantasize sizzling woks and bubbling, fragrant steamers. My shock, of course, was evident as I sat down to a feast of whole chicken that had been microwaved.

And yes, it was delicious! It even resembled the Chinese "beggar's chicken" that remains moist and tender because it is cooked in a clay pot. But the dish was less than perfect. The chicken was cooked with the skin, which was soggy and unattractive.

The moral here is that microwaving poultry is a good way to keep it moist and tender without a lot of extra fat and calories. By removing the skin you solve the problem of aesthetics and even avoid adding more fat to your diet. (You'll also want to trim off other excess fat or it will pop and spatter during microwaving.)

Texture- and taste-wise, boneless, skinless breasts (chicken cutlets) microwave the best of all poultry. Skinless dark meat, which takes about 30 seconds per pound (450 g) longer than white, is good but not great. The texture of the flesh is coarser and somewhat irregular and it will be slightly tough. Boneless, skinless turkey, which has the coarsest flesh of all, can be microwaved but is quite chewy. The recipes in this chapter are best made with chicken cutlets, but if your taste is for dark meat or turkey, they still work well enough. Cutting the flesh against the grain (when the recipe calls for strips or pieces) helps make the texture tender.

More Poultry Pointers

Add these tips to your microwaving repertoire for perfect microwaved poultry.

- Smaller pieces of poultry will be more tender than larger ones and they may be safer, too. Research has revealed that microwaving is less effective than conventional cooking for destroying salmonella and staph organisms. Because microwaves don't penetrate to the center of a big bird, it's best to roast the Thanksgiving turkey in the oven. But if you absolutely must microwave a whole bird, use a thermometer to make sure the internal temperature remains 170°F (77°C) for 30 minutes after you remove it from the microwave. To maintain this temperature, you may have to keep the bird warm in a conventional oven.
- Pounding chicken cutlets so they're of equal thickness will help them cook evenly. One way is to set the cutlets between two sheets of waxed paper and pound them with the bottom of a sauté pan.

FRICASSEE OF CHICKEN WITH FRESH BASIL

4 servings • 170 calories per serving

1 lb	chicken cutlets, cut into 1-inch (2.5-cm) pieces	450 g
3	plum tomatoes, peeled and chopped	
2	cloves garlic, thinly sliced	
¼ cup	minced leeks	60 ml
2 Tbs	chicken stock	30 ml
3	bay leaves	
1 tsp	olive oil	5 ml
2 Tbs	minced fresh basil	30 ml
1 Tbs	light cream or milk	15 ml

Scoop the chicken into a 9-inch (23-cm) glass pie dish and cover with vented plastic wrap. Microwave on full power until the chicken is cooked through, 4½ to 5 minutes, stopping to stir midway.

Remove the chicken with a slotted spoon and drain off any liquid. Combine the tomatoes, garlic, leeks, stock, bay leaves and oil in the same dish. Cover with vented plastic wrap and microwave on full power for 2 to 2½ minutes, stirring once midway.

Immediately stir in the chicken, basil and cream or milk and let stand for 4 minutes. Remove bay leaves and serve hot in shallow bowls.

Snazzy Saffron Sauce

Jazz up a sauce or dressing for chicken salad with saffron. The rich color will make you think you're eating something far more fattening than you really are.

In a small bowl combine a pinch of crushed saffron threads with 2 tablespoons (30 ml) of milk. Cover with vented plastic wrap and microwave on full power for about 1 minute. Let stand for another minute before adding to plain, low-fat yogurt or stock-based sauces or dressings.

CIRCASSIAN CHICKEN

Here's a famous Turkish dish with the calories slashed. Serve it with rice and fresh fruit.

4 servings • 180 calories per serving

1 Tbs	tahini (sesame paste)	15 ml
1 tsp	freshly squeezed lemon juice	5 ml
2	cloves garlic, minced	
½ tsp	thyme	2 ml
1 lb	chicken cutlets, cut into 4 pieces and pounded lightly	450 g
½ tsp	paprika	2 ml
1 Tbs	olive oil	15 ml

Combine the tahini, lemon juice, garlic and thyme in a small bowl. Rub the mixture into the chicken pieces, then set them around the edge of a 9-inch (23-cm) glass pie dish. Cover loosely with crumpled waxed paper and microwave on full power until cooked through, 6½ to 7 minutes. Refrigerate until chilled.

When you're ready, combine the paprika and olive oil in a small dish. Cover with vented plastic wrap and microwave on full power until heated through and fragrant, 40 to 60 seconds.

Meanwhile, arrange the chicken pieces on a serving platter. When the paprika mixture is ready, give it a stir and pour it over the chicken in a pretty design. Serve cold.

CHICKEN SCALLOPINI WITH TOMATO BUTTER AND ZITI

If you can't find fresh, ripe plum tomatoes, use canned ones.

4 servings • 294 calories per serving

8	plum tomatoes, peeled, seeded and juiced		
1 Tbs	sweet butter, softened	15 ml
1	cinnamon stick	
1	bay leaf	
	olive oil for painting, if necessary	
½ lb	chicken cutlets, cut into 4 pieces and pounded lightly	225 g
	olive oil for rubbing	
2 cups	cooked ziti	480 ml
	freshly grated Parmesan for tossing	

Scoop the tomatoes into a processor or blender along with the butter and whiz until smooth.

Pour the tomato mixture into a 9-inch (23-cm) glass pie dish and add the cinnamon stick and bay leaf. Microwave on full power, uncovered, until thickened and reduced in volume, about 8 minutes. Let stand while you prepare the chicken.

Preheat a browning dish according to manufacturer's instructions, which will probably be 4 to 6½ minutes. If the browning dish has a surface that may stick, paint a bit of oil on it after it's been preheated.

Rub the chicken with a bit of olive oil. When the browning dish is ready, set the chicken pieces on it and microwave uncovered according to manufacturer's instructions or about 1½ minutes on each side.

In a large bowl toss together the tomato butter (cinnamon stick and bay leaf removed), chicken, ziti and Parmesan. Serve in shallow bowls, making sure each person gets a piece of chicken.

CHICKEN OREGANO WITH SPAGHETTI

4 servings • 244 calories per serving

Toss the onion rings into a 9-inch (23-cm) glass pie dish and sprinkle with the olive oil. Cover with vented plastic wrap and microwave on full power for 2 minutes.

Toss the chicken into the dish along with the lemon, garlic and oregano. Cover with vented plastic wrap and microwave

1	onion, sliced and separated into rings	
1 tsp	olive oil	5 ml
¾ lb	chicken cutlets, cut into 1-inch (2.5-cm) pieces	340 g
	juice and pulp of ½ lemon	
2	cloves garlic, finely minced	
1 tsp	oregano	5 ml
2 cups	cooked spaghetti	480 ml
	freshly grated Parmesan for tossing	
	minced fresh parsley for tossing	

on full power until the chicken is cooked through and the onions have softened, about 6 minutes.

Immediately toss with the spaghetti, Parmesan and parsley and let stand for a couple of minutes before serving hot.

Hot Pepper Butter

Serve with poached, grilled or microwaved chicken. And if you have them on hand, warm tortillas are a nice accompaniment.

*Makes enough for 1 lb of chicken •
108 calories per recipe*

1 Tbs	sweet butter	15 ml
	juice and pulp of ½ lemon	
½ tsp	hot pepper sauce, or to taste	2 ml
1 tsp	finely minced jalapeño peppers (wear plastic gloves when handling)	5 ml

Combine all of the ingredients in a small bowl and cover with vented plastic wrap. Microwave on full power until the butter has melted, about 1½ minutes.

LOW-FAT GRILLED CHICKEN

Here's a way to use your microwave to keep skinless chicken moist when grilling.

4 servings • 145 calories per serving

1 lb	chicken cutlets, cut into 4 pieces	450 g
1 tsp	tarragon	5 ml
3	allspice berries	
1 tsp	coriander seeds	5 ml
1 tsp	cumin seeds	5 ml
pinch	turmeric	
¼ tsp	dried red pepper flakes	1 ml
1 tsp	grated lemon peel	5 ml
1 Tbs	honey	15 ml

Arrange the chicken around the edge of a 9-inch (23-cm) glass pie dish and set aside.

In a spice grinder or mortar, grind the tarragon, allspice, coriander, cumin, turmeric, pepper flakes and lemon peel.

In a small bowl combine the spice mixture with the honey. Then rub it into the chicken. Cover with vented plastic wrap and microwave on full power for about 2½ minutes.

Grill over hot coals until golden and cooked through. Chicken cutlets of natural thickness will need 5 to 6 minutes of grilling on each side. Ones that have been pounded will take about 3 minutes per side.

CHICKEN WITH CASHEWS AND BROCCOLI

Serve warm with rice or chilled with romaine petals for scooping.

4 servings • 205 calories per serving

1 lb	chicken cutlets, cut into equal bite-size pieces	450 g
1 tsp	peanut oil	5 ml
2	cloves garlic, minced	
2 Tbs	hoisin sauce*	30 ml
2 Tbs	chicken stock	30 ml
pinch	Chinese five spice powder*	
1 cup	chopped cooked broccoli	240 ml
¼ cup	chopped raw cashews	60 ml
3	scallions, chopped	

Scoop the chicken into a 9-inch (23-cm) glass pie dish and set aside.

In a small bowl mix together the oil, garlic, hoisin sauce, stock and five spice powder. Pour over the chicken and combine well. Cover with vented plastic wrap and microwave on full power until the chicken has cooked through, about 6 minutes.

Immediately stir in the broccoli, cashews and scallions and let stand uncovered for about 4 minutes.

*Hoisin sauce and Chinese five spice powder are available at Oriental markets and many supermarkets.

Ground Turkey

It's important to buy turkey meat and grind it yourself in a processor or meat grinder. That way you know exactly what's in it and can be sure there's no fatty skin. White turkey meat contains fewer calories than dark, but the difference is small, so create whatever blend you have a taste for.

To cook, arrange 1 pound (450 g) of ground turkey in a 9-inch (23-cm) glass pie dish, cover with vented plastic wrap and microwave on full power until cooked through, about 6 minutes (stir or shake midway). Drain if necessary, then let stand for about 4 minutes before using in chili, in stuffings for sweet peppers or globe onions and in soups or stews.

Rapid Rabbit

You're right, rabbit is not a bird, but it's comparable to chicken in so many culinary respects that this is the ideal place to present it.

Rabbit is a pale, cream-colored meat that's tender and smooth. The taste is country, not gamey, and it may remind you of grass-fed veal.

In terms of health, rabbit comes skinless and is lower in fat and calories than roasted chicken.

Rabbit is available through many poultry purveyors, but plan ahead because you may need to order in advance. Ask the butcher to cut the back, which, unlike chicken, has lots of nice meat, into 3 pieces. It's easier to microwave and handle that way.

To microwave a 2-pound (1-kg) rabbit, arrange the pieces around the rim of a large, glass pie dish. The meaty parts of the legs should point out and the bony parts should point toward the middle. Tuck the thin sides of the saddle (mid-back) under the thicker part so they don't overcook. Cover with vented plastic wrap and microwave on full power until cooked through, 10 to 13 minutes. Rotate the dish and flip the pieces midway. Let stand for about 5 minutes before serving.

Flavoring Ideas

- Sprinkle with chopped wild mushrooms, bay leaves and dry white wine before microwaving
- Cover with chopped tomatoes, chopped onions, chopped green peppers and thyme before microwaving.
- Rub the pieces with a mixture of Dijon-style and coarse mustards and sprinkle with minced shallots and thyme before microwaving
- Pour on a mixture of dry red wine, bay leaf, garlic, parsley and tarragon, then microwave
- Microwave the rabbit, let cool, then shred the meat with your fingers and use in a chicken salad recipe

Heating Tortillas

Wrap four soft flour tortillas in damp paper towels and microwave on full power until heated through, about a minute. Fill with shredded cooked chicken, avocado slices and chopped ripe tomatoes.

Unfried Onions

Many recipes for sautéed chicken require minced onions that have been sautéed in fat. You can avoid that fat by using your microwave.

Scoop 2 tablespoons (30 ml) of minced onions into a small dish and cover with vented plastic wrap. Microwave on full power until tender, about 1½ minutes. The onions will be sweet and flavorful.

HAPPY FAMILY PANCAKE

The Chinese are clever when naming their foods. For instance, a recipe that includes chicken and eggs might be referred to as Happy Family. A recipe that includes pork and eggs might be called Strangers and Children.

Happy Family Pancake will remind you of Egg Foo Yong, except it's not fried.

½ lb	chicken cutlets, sliced into small pieces	225 g
¼ cup	chopped mushrooms	60 ml
1 cup	mung bean sprouts	240 ml
3	scallions, minced	
4	eggs, beaten	
splash	light soy sauce	
3 Tbs	oyster sauce*	45 ml
1 Tbs	chicken stock	15 ml

4 servings • 161 calories per serving

Scoop the chicken into a 9-inch (23-cm) glass pie dish. Cover with vented plastic wrap and microwave on full power until cooked through, about 3 minutes. Drain off any liquid and let stand while you prepare the rest of the ingredients.

Sprinkle the mushrooms in with the chicken. Pat the bean sprouts dry and add them and the scallions, too.

In a medium bowl, beat together the eggs, soy sauce and a splash of water and pour the mixture over the chicken and veggies. Cover with vented plastic wrap and microwave on medium power until set, about 7 minutes, rotating the dish several times. To check for doneness, lift the dish and peek at the bottom through the glass. If there's still some moisture, it's not done. Let stand while you prepare the sauce.

Combine the oyster sauce and stock in a small dish and cover with vented plastic wrap. Microwave on full power until thin, dark and liquidy, 1½ to 2 minutes. Serve with wedges of the pancake.

*Oyster sauce is a dark and pungent condiment, available at Oriental markets and many supermarkets.

GINGER CHICKEN BUNDLES

When halved or sliced into disks, the color contrast of the green outside and white inside is interesting. Serve on a hill of fragrant rice, like basmati.

4 servings • 196 calories per serving

1	lb	chicken cutlets	450 g
¾	tsp	finely minced fresh ginger	3 ml
2		cloves garlic, finely minced	
¼	cup	finely minced sweet onions	60 ml
1	Tbs	*nam pla** or light soy sauce	15 ml
2	Tbs	toasted sesame seeds	30 ml
16		broccoli rabe leaves	
		toasted sesame oil for sprinkling	

Combine the chicken, ginger, garlic, onions, *nam pla* or soy sauce and sesame seeds in a processor and use on/off pulses until the chicken is ground and the mixture is well combined.

Rinse the broccoli rabe leaves and wrap them, still wet, in a couple of paper towels. Microwave wrapped leaves on full power until just tender, about 30 seconds. Remove leaves from towels.

Set a slight tablespoon of chicken mixture on the stem edge of a leaf. Fold in the sides and roll up into a bundle. Repeat with the remaining leaves.

Arrange half of the bundles along the rim of a large dinner plate and cover with vented plastic wrap. Microwave on full power for about 6 minutes. Let stand while you repeat microwaving with the rest of the bundles. Let them stand for 4 minutes, then serve warm or chilled, sprinkled with the sesame oil.

*Nam pla is a dark, flavorful and pungent, fish-based sauce that's available at Oriental markets and specialty foods stores.

PICNIC CHICKEN FROM JAPAN

4 servings • 128 calories per serving

handful	dried lemongrass or 1 tsp (5 ml) dried lemon peel	
1 lb	chicken cutlets, cut into 4 pieces and pounded lightly	450 g
1 tsp	light soy sauce	5 ml
2 tsp	rice vinegar	10 ml
1	clove garlic, finely minced	
½ tsp	finely minced ginger	2 ml
splash	toasted sesame oil	
	minced scallions for sprinkling	
	romaine petals for rolling	

Sprinkle the lemongrass or lemon peel in the bottom of a microwave-safe ring pan. Arrange the chicken in the pan.

In a small bowl combine the soy sauce, vinegar, garlic, ginger and sesame oil. Pour it over the chicken, covering it well. Cover the pan with vented plastic wrap and microwave on full power until the chicken has cooked through, 5 to 5½ minutes, rotating the pan midway.

Refrigerate the chicken until cool. Discard the lemongrass, and use your fingers to shred each piece of chicken into 3 or 4 pieces.

Arrange the chicken pieces on a serving platter and sprinkle with scallions. To eat, set some chicken in a romaine petal, roll and enjoy.

Currying Flavor

Commercial curry powders, and home-ground for that matter, should be heated before they are eaten or they'll taste raw. Microwaving is a good way to heat these spice blends without using fat.

Simply pour 2 teaspoons (10 ml) of curry powder into a small, glass dish and microwave, uncovered, on full power until fragrant, about 1 minute. Let stand for another minute before adding, according to taste, to dressings for poultry salads or to a cooked sauce that needs some snap.

CHICKEN WITH STARFRUIT AND CHILIES

Shrimp powder, famous in many Asian cuisines, is available from Oriental markets and specialty foods stores. At first, you may think it's out of your way, but try some and you'll realize it's worth the trip. Shrimp powder is a super salt substitute, particularly when used in marinades, sauces and soups.

4 servings • 141 calories per serving

1	large or 2 small starfruit* juice and pulp of ½ lime	
2	cloves garlic, minced	
splash	hot pepper sauce, or to taste	
pinch	shrimp powder	
splash	light soy sauce	
3	dried, hot, Asian-type chili peppers	
1 lb	chicken cutlets, cut into 4 pieces and pounded lightly	450 g
2 Tbs	finely minced sweet red peppers	30 ml
2 Tbs	finely minced green peppers	30 ml

Chop enough of the starfruit to press through a garlic press (you want the pulp, too) until you have ¼ cup (60 ml) juice. Add the lime, garlic, hot pepper sauce, shrimp powder, soy sauce and chilies.

Set the chicken in a 9-inch (23-cm) glass pie dish and pour the starfruit mixture over it, tucking the chilies underneath the chicken. Cover and marinate, refrigerated, for at least an hour. This is a good recipe to put together in the morning and when you're ready for dinner, it's done.

Arrange the chicken around the rim of the dish, cover with vented plastic wrap and microwave on full power until the chicken is cooked through, about 5 minutes. Flip the pieces midway.

*Starfruit, or carambola, is cylinder shaped with 4 to 6 ribs that run vertically. When sliced it looks like bright golden stars. It's popular in the cuisines of southeast Asia and the West Indies and is usually eaten raw in salads, as a flavoring for beverages or in jams and jellies. The Old Manor, a lovely inn on the island of Nevis, serves a great starfruit pie and wonderful starfruit daiquiris.

(continued)

Meanwhile, slice the rest of the starfruit. Let the chicken stand for 4 minutes before sprinkling with the minced peppers (if you wish, thinly sliced peppers may be used) and starfruit slices. If you like, run the chicken under the broiler until a bit of golden color appears, before adding the peppers and starfruit.

Coconut by Microwave

To prepare a coconut for eating, first find the softest of its three eyes. Then pierce that eye with a screwdriver and whack it with a hammer. Continue to whack until the eye is pierced completely through and the coconut just begins to crack.

Drain the juice and reserve it for adding to marinades for chicken or fish or to replace some of the liquid in puddings.

Wrap the coconut in plastic wrap and microwave on full power until fragrant and very hot, about 5 minutes. Let it stand for 15 minutes, then whack it hard with the hammer until it splits.

Use a sturdy knife to pry the meat out, and peel off the outer brown part, if you like.

Grate and use as needed in desserts, tropical chicken salads and in Brazilian, southeast Asian and West Indian recipes. Store it tightly covered in the refrigerator or make Unsweetened Coconut Milk.

Unsweetened Coconut Milk

Makes ½ cup • 93 calories per recipe

1 Tbs	finely grated coconut meat	15 ml
½ cup	low-fat milk, whole milk or light cream	120 ml

In a small bowl combine the coconut and milk or cream. Cover with vented plastic wrap and microwave on medium power until fragrant, about 1½ minutes.

Store tightly covered in the refrigerator for about a week. The longer it sits, the richer the flavor will be, which is especially nice if you've used low-fat milk. Strain before using.

In case you're wondering what coconut is doing here instead of in the dessert chapter, check out the recipe for Chicken with Coconut Curry *(Adobo)* on the next page.

CHICKEN WITH COCONUT CURRY (ADOBO)

You'll find variations of this theme in the cuisines of the Philippines and the Caribbean. This version contains a mere splash of oil and absolutely no salt.

4 servings • 277 calories per serving

1 lb	chicken cutlets, sliced into thin strips	450 g
1 tsp	peanut oil	5 ml
1 tsp	light soy sauce	5 ml
1 Tbs	freshly squeezed lime juice	15 ml
1 Tbs	red wine vinegar	15 ml
½ cup	Unsweetened Coconut Milk (page 151)*	120 ml
¼ tsp	hot pepper sauce, or to taste	1 ml
¼ tsp	minced fresh ginger	1 ml
2 tsp	honey	10 ml
½ tsp	coriander seeds, crushed	2 ml
1 tsp	cornstarch	5 ml
¼ cup	coarsely chopped raw cashews	60 ml
2 Tbs	finely minced fresh parsley	30 ml
2	scallions, minced	
	cooked rice or skinny noodles for serving	

Toss the chicken into a 9-inch (23-cm) glass pie dish with the oil, soy sauce, lime juice and vinegar. Cover and let marinate for at least an hour.

When you're ready, push the chicken strips away from the center of the dish so they'll cook evenly. Cover with vented plastic wrap and microwave on full power until the chicken has cooked through, about 5½ minutes, rotating the dish midway. Let it stand while you prepare the sauce.

In a 1-quart (1-liter) dish combine the coconut milk, hot pepper sauce, ginger, honey, coriander and cornstarch. Cover with vented plastic wrap and microwave on medium power until thickened, about 3 minutes.

Drain the chicken and toss with the sauce, cashews, parsley and scallions. Serve hot with cooked rice or skinny noodles.

*Unsweetened coconut milk is also available at East Indian markets.

MUSTARD-POACHED CHICKEN WITH ZUCCHINI RELISH

4 servings • 150 calories per serving

1 lb	chicken cutlets, cut into 4 pieces	450 g
1 tsp	Dijon-style mustard	5 ml
Zucchini Relish		
1	small zucchini, sliced	
2	scallions, chopped	
2 tsp	sweet butter	10 ml
½ cup	fresh spinach, stems removed	120 ml
pinch	cayenne pepper or other ground red pepper	
pinch	freshly grated nutmeg	
	minced fresh chives for sprinkling	

Rub the chicken with the mustard and arrange the pieces around the edge of a 9-inch (23-cm) glass pie dish. Cover with vented plastic wrap and microwave on full power until the chicken has cooked through, about 5½ minutes. Flip the pieces midway. Let the chicken stand while you prepare the relish.

For the Zucchini Relish, combine the zucchini, scallions and butter in another 9-inch (23-cm) glass pie dish. Cover with vented plastic wrap and microwave on full power until the veggies are tender, about 3 minutes.

Scoop the veggies into a processor or blender and add the spinach, cayenne or other red pepper and nutmeg. Whiz until smooth.

Serve the chicken warm or chilled, sprinkled with chives and with relish on the side.

HONEY CHICKEN ON RICE

Traditionally, the chicken is coated with a spicy batter, then deep-fried and tossed with honey. This version omits the deep frying but not the flavor.

4 servings • 231 calories per serving

In a 9-inch (23-cm) glass pie dish combine the thyme, garlic, Worcestershire, hot pepper sauce, oil, dried pepper flakes, paprika and lime.

Toss the chicken with the spice mixture. Spread the chicken out in a ring shape so it cooks evenly. Then cover with vented plastic wrap and microwave on full power until the chicken has cooked through, about 6 minutes. Rotate the dish midway.

Immediately toss with the honey and let stand for about 4 minutes. Serve hot with the rice, sprinkled with parsley.

1 tsp	thyme	5 ml
2	cloves garlic, finely minced	
2 tsp	Worcestershire sauce	10 ml
1 tsp	hot pepper sauce, or to taste	5 ml
1 tsp	peanut oil	5 ml
½ tsp	dried red pepper flakes, or to taste	2 ml
¾ tsp	sweet paprika	3 ml
	juice and pulp of 1 lime	
1 lb	chicken cutlets, cut into equal bite-size pieces	450 g
2 tsp	honey	10 ml
1½ cups	cooked rice	360 ml
	minced fresh parsley for sprinkling	

CHICKEN WITH APRICOTS AND ROSEMARY

4 servings • 167 calories per serving

2 tsp	sweet butter	10 ml
2 Tbs	freshly squeezed lemon juice	30 ml
¼ cup	minced dried apricots	60 ml
1 tsp	minced fresh rosemary	5 ml
1 lb	chicken cutlets, cut into 4 pieces and pounded lightly	450 g
	minced fresh chives for sprinkling	

Thai Glaze

A no-fat-added, no-salt-added glaze for roasting whole or quartered chicken. It can also be used as a marinade.

Makes enough to glaze 1 bird • 46 calories per recipe

1 tsp	tamarind paste*	5 ml
½ tsp	very finely minced fresh ginger	2 ml
1	clove garlic, very finely minced	
	juice and pulp of 1 orange	
1 tsp	light soy sauce	5 ml
1 tsp	very finely minced fresh mint	5 ml

Combine all of the ingredients in a small dish and don't worry if the tamarind doesn't dissolve, it will later. Cover with vented plastic wrap and microwave on full power until fragrant, about 1 minute.

*Tamarind paste comes from tropical tamarind pods and tastes like a combination of molasses and lemon. It's available at Oriental markets, East Indian markets and specialty foods stores.

Combine the butter, lemon juice, apricots and rosemary in a 9-inch (23-cm) glass pie dish, cover with vented plastic wrap and microwave on full power until the butter has melted, about 2 minutes.

Toss the chicken in the apricot mixture, then arrange it around the rim of the dish, cover and microwave on full power until the chicken has cooked through, about 6½ minutes. Rotate the dish and flip the chicken midway.

Let stand for about 4 minutes. To serve, arrange the chicken on a heated platter, scoop the apricot mixture over it, then sprinkle with the chives.

TERRINES
OF CHICKEN
WITH LEEKS

Serve warm or chilled with crusty bread and mustards.

4 servings • 217 calories per serving

1 lb	chicken cutlets	450 g
1	large leek, finely minced	
2 tsp	Dijon-style mustard	10 ml
1 tsp	tarragon	5 ml
pinch	mace	
2	eggs	
	olive oil for rubbing, optional	

Combine the chicken, leeks, mustard, tarragon, mace and eggs in a processor or blender and, with on/off pulses, whiz the mixture until the chicken is ground into small pieces but stop before it's pureed.

Scoop the mixture into 4 cups, ramekins or small dishes, press in and level off the tops. Microwave, uncovered, on full power, until set, about 7 minutes, rotating the cups twice. Let stand for 5 minutes before unmolding.

If desired, rub the unmolded terrines with olive oil and run under the broiler or a browning unit until mottled with brown.

CHICKEN STUFFED WITH ASPARAGUS AND SCALLIONS

Serve with a salad of spring lettuces and fresh strawberries for dessert.

4 servings • 140 calories per serving

1 tsp	Dijon-style mustard	5 ml
1	clove garlic, chopped	
½ tsp	thyme	2 ml
2 Tbs	freshly squeezed lemon juice	30 ml
1 lb	chicken cutlets, cut into 4 pieces and pounded until very thin	450 g
8	asparagus spears	
4	scallions	

In a spice grinder or mortar, make a paste of the mustard, garlic, thyme and lemon juice. Lay the chicken pieces out flat and coat the exposed sides with the paste.

Snap the tough ends off of the asparagus, peel and slice into thin strips or ribbons. Cut the roots off the scallions and slice into thin strips or ribbons. Divide the asparagus and scallions into 4 bundles and set each on the long end of each chicken piece. Then roll up.

Wrap each roll in plastic wrap and arrange around the edges of a dinner plate, seam side down. Microwave on full power for 6 to 7 minutes. Let stand for 5 minutes, remove plastic wrap then slice into sections and serve hot or chilled.

Note: Dijon-style mustard is a nice accompaniment, as is Zucchini Relish, page 153.

Marinade of Pungent Peppercorns

Here's a no-fat-added, no-salt-added marinade for poultry or rabbit: In a mortar, mash 1 teaspoon (5 ml) of green peppercorns. Combine in a small bowl with 2 tablespoons (30 ml) of champagne vinegar (or other mild white vinegar). Cover with vented plastic wrap and microwave on full power for about 1½ minutes. Watch to make sure it doesn't boil. Rub on poultry or rabbit and let marinate for an hour before grilling.

Chicken the Easy Way

Start with a pound of chicken cutlets, trimmed of excess fat. If they're not all the same thickness, pound them until they are.

Next, arrange the chicken in a microwave-safe ring pan and sprinkle on a bit of lemon juice, lime juice, dry white wine or a particular herb that will fit into your cooking scheme. Lemon juice and tarragon are nice together.

Cover with vented plastic wrap and microwave on full power until the chicken is cooked through, about 6 minutes. The ring pan helps the chicken cook evenly. Let stand for several minutes, then use in any recipe requiring cooked chicken or serve chilled with an array of condiments like mustards and chutneys. You can also stash the chicken away in the refrigerator and slice it for sandwiches. Or, create a chicken salad.

Ideas for Chicken Salads

Use your fingers to tear cooked chicken into shreds. Then toss with:

- Minced dried apricots and raisins, minced ginger, minced garlic and a splash of toasted sesame oil.
- Cooked rice, tender asparagus tips, basil, thyme and a splash of fragrant olive oil
- Pecan halves, minced red onions, chopped artichoke bottoms, oregano, lemon juice and a splash of hazelnut oil
- Corn kernels, chopped ripe tomatoes, minced garlic, minced jalapeño peppers (wear plastic gloves when handling), minced fresh coriander, lime juice and olive oil
- Minced dried tomatoes, minced fresh mint, lemon juice and a splash of light cream

Defatting Duck

Begin with about a 5-lb (2.5-kg) duck. If you have a lean breed, like Muscovy, you'll have even less fat to remove. Use poultry shears to cut the duck into pieces (or have the butcher do it) discarding the back and wings. Look for the excess fat, especially around the neck, and trim it off.

Set the pieces in a microwave-safe drainer with a bottom container to catch the fat. Cover and microwave on full power for 7 to 10 minutes. Let stand for 5 minutes so the fat can continue to drip. You'll be amazed at the amount of fat in the container. One time I measured a cup!

For the tastiest of ducks, rub a marinade on the defatted pieces and let them marinate for a couple of hours or overnight.

Ideas for Marinades

- Equal parts of honey and prepared horseradish
- Equal parts of prepared mustard and apricot jam
- Hoisin sauce
- Buttermilk and crushed fresh herbs like thyme and basil

When you're ready, roast the duck pieces in a 400°F (204°C) oven for 30 to 40 minutes, using a drip pan to catch any fat that's left.

CHICKEN WITH DRIED TOMATOES AND TINY PASTA

4 servings • 239 calories per serving

1 Tbs	sweet butter	15 ml
1	clove garlic, finely minced	
½ tsp	marjoram	2 ml
3	bay leaves	
5	dried tomatoes, minced	
2 Tbs	chicken stock	30 ml
¾ lb	chicken cutlets, cut into equal bite-size pieces	340 g
1 cup	cooked tiny pasta, like orzo	240 ml
	minced scallions for tossing	

Combine the butter, garlic, marjoram, bay leaves, tomatoes and stock in a 9-inch (23-cm) glass pie dish and cover with vented plastic wrap. Microwave on full power until the butter has melted, about 1 minute.

Meanwhile, add the chicken pieces to the dish and toss well, then push the chicken to the sides of the dish, leaving the center open. This will help it cook evenly. Cover and microwave until the chicken has cooked through, about 4½ minutes. Let stand for 2 minutes.

Remove bay leaves, then toss with the pasta and scallions and serve warm.

CHICKEN WITH GRAPEFRUIT

Choose the color grapefruit you prefer, but be aware that pink contains far more vitamin C than yellow.

4 servings • 165 calories per serving

	juice and pulp of 1 grapefruit	
1 tsp	Dijon-style mustard	5 ml
3 Tbs	minced fresh basil	45 ml
1 lb	chicken cutlets, sliced into thin strips	450 g
	olive oil for painting, if necessary	
½ tsp	cornstarch	2 ml
	fresh grapefruit sections for serving	

Combine the grapefruit juice and pulp, mustard and basil in a 9-inch (23-cm) glass pie dish and toss in the chicken. Let marinate for about an hour.

When you're ready, preheat a browning dish according to manufacturer's instructions, which should be about 5 minutes. (If it doesn't have a nonstick surface, paint with a bit of oil after preheating.) Microwave the chicken strips (minus marinade), uncovered, on full power for about 3 minutes, flipping midway. Let stand while you prepare the sauce.

Whisk the cornstarch into the marinade and microwave uncovered until thick and bubbly, 3 to 4 minutes, stirring every minute. Pour over the chicken and serve with grapefruit sections.

NEW WAVE MEATS

Before the fitness craze hit, the typical American was a tad overweight—and not too worried about it. But the American of today has a new, fit body—trimmer, with more muscle and less fat. And the same is true for today's meat. So, if you want to be part of the in-crowd, the meat you'll eat will be *lean*.

Start by buying meat from a butcher who follows the "quarter-inch-trim" policy, which means that only ¼ inch of excess fat is left on meat, as opposed to the ½ inch that was popular for years. You still may have to trim a bit more fat off at home, but these "quarter-inch-trim" butchers are generally more aware of lean meats and many even buy leaner breeds of cattle and pork. Longhorn, for instance, is one lean cattle breed that you should look for.

Lean meat is perfect for microwaving because it cooks faster and remains juicier without added fat. Ribbons and slices of meat microwave exceptionally well because they cook more evenly and with more tender results than large hunks. And they may be safer, too—the USDA suggests that during microwaving, big bones can shield surrounding meat from cooking through. Besides, roasts are at their least palatable when microwaved. If you want roast beef, roast it.

Love-Meat-Tender Tips

To get a finished product you'll be proud to serve, follow these tips:

- For maximum tenderness always slice meat against its grain.
- Never salt meat before microwaving because it draws out moisture.
- Here's a trick that will give maximum flavor to microwaved stews. Assemble ingredients ahead of time, liquid and all, and refrigerate overnight. Or assemble in the morning before you leave for work. Microwave when you're ready to eat and the flavors will be well acquainted and bold.
- Cover stew-type dishes with a layer of foil, then cover with vented plastic wrap on top. The foil directs microwaves to the bottom of the dish and helps the liquid simmer. It also protects the top pieces from drying out. And no, foil used in this way won't hurt your microwave.
- The USDA recommends that you check the finished temperature of microwaved pork with a thermometer. It should read 170°F (77°C).
- Many of the recipes in this chapter, especially those in which the meat is sliced into ribbons, can be microwaved on a browning dish. Browning dishes can sear meat, sealing in juices and adding textural interest. Follow the manufacturer's instructions, which are normally to preheat the dish for at least 4 minutes.
- Browning dishes without nonstick surfaces will need to be painted with a bit of oil after preheating, before the meat goes on. Use something flavorful like olive oil or peanut oil, depending on the character of the recipe. Also, don't cover the meat or it will steam instead of sear.

KOREAN SESAME BEEF

*If you love garlic, Korean cuisine will appeal to you. Here's a no-oil-added version of flavorful **Bul-kogee**. It is delicious with steamed rice and blanched Chinese peas.*

4 servings • 192 calories per serving

1 Tbs	toasted sesame seeds	15 ml
3	cloves garlic, finely minced	
½ tsp	minced fresh ginger	2 ml
2	scallions, very finely minced	
1 tsp	light soy sauce	5 ml
1 tsp	honey	5 ml
1 tsp	freshly squeezed lemon juice	5 ml
1 lb	lean top round, sirloin or rib steak, sliced against the grain into very thin ribbons	450 g

In a 9-inch (23-cm) glass pie dish combine the sesame seeds, garlic, ginger, scallions, soy sauce, honey and lemon juice.

Toss the beef well with the marinade. Let marinate for at least an hour.

When you're ready to eat, spread the beef out in the dish, cover with vented plastic wrap and microwave on full power until cooked through the way you like it, 5 to 6 minutes for medium rare (stir the beef a couple of times during cooking). Let stand for about 2 minutes before serving.

Variation: You may use lean pork instead of beef but marinate for at least 2 hours and increase the microwaving time by about 1 minute.

Browning Dish Note: Follow manufacturer's instructions, or preheat a nonstick browning dish for about 5 minutes, spread the beef out on it and microwave, uncovered, on full power (flipping every minute) until done the way you like it, 2½ to 3 minutes for medium rare.

BEEF WITH RED CURRY PASTE

Serve this Thai dish with hot rice and chilled orange sections.

4 servings • 199 calories per serving

Combine the chili, hot pepper sauce, onions, garlic, scallions, ginger, *nam pla* or soy sauce, coriander, lime peel, tomatoes and oil in a processor or blender and whiz until you have a smooth and well-combined paste.

Tip the beef into a 9-inch (23-cm) glass pie dish. Scoop in the paste and toss until all the ribbons of beef are coated. Then let marinate for at least an hour.

When you're ready to eat, spread the beef out in the dish. Cover with vented plastic wrap and microwave on full power until it's done the way you like it, about 5 minutes for medium rare (stir the beef a couple of times during cooking). Let stand for about 2 minutes before you sprinkle with the mint or basil and serve hot.

Variation: Substitute lamb for the beef.

Browning Dish Note: Follow manufacturer's instructions, or preheat a nonstick browning dish for about 5 minutes.

1	small, fresh, hot chili pepper, seeded and ribs removed	
5	drops hot pepper sauce, or to taste	
⅓ cup	chopped onions	80 ml
2	cloves garlic, minced	
1	scallion, minced	
½ tsp	minced fresh ginger	2 ml
1½ tsp	*nam pla** or light soy sauce	7 ml
½ tsp	coriander seeds, ground	2 ml
¼ tsp	grated lime peel	1 ml
2	medium tomatoes, peeled and juiced	
1 tsp	peanut oil	5 ml
1 lb	lean top round or sirloin, sliced against the grain into very thin ribbons	450 g
	minced fresh mint or basil for sprinkling	

Spread the beef out and microwave, uncovered, on full power (flipping every minute) until done the way you like it, about 2½ minutes for medium rare.

Nam pla is a dark, flavorful and pungent, fish-based sauce that's available at Oriental markets and specialty foods stores.

Ginger Chicken Bundles (page 148)

Picnic Chicken from Japan (page 149)

Chicken with Starfruit and Chilies (page 150)

Chicken with Apricots and Rosemary (page 155)

St. Joe Ribs in a Bag (page 181)

Marinated Stuffed Beef *(Matambre),* page 184

Veal with Dried Tomatoes and Mozzarella (page 185)

Soft Tortillas with *Piccadillo* Filling (page 187)

SKEWERED BEEF IN PEANUT SAUCE

Serve with short-grained rice and tenderly cooked green beans.

4 servings • 242 calories per serving

3 Tbs	peanut butter	45 ml
¼ tsp	hot pepper sauce, or to taste	1 ml
2 Tbs	freshly squeezed lemon juice	30 ml
¼ tsp	minced fresh ginger	1 ml
1 tsp	molasses	5 ml
splash	light soy sauce	
1 lb	lean top round, thinly sliced into ribbons finely minced fresh chives for rolling	450 g

In a small bowl combine the peanut butter, hot pepper sauce, lemon juice, ginger, molasses and soy sauce. Cover with vented plastic wrap and microwave on full power until the peanut butter has softened, 20 to 30 seconds.

Toss the beef into the peanut sauce until all the pieces are well coated. Save any extra sauce. Then thread the slices onto 6-inch (15-cm) bamboo skewers, but don't crowd them. Roll the skewers in the chives, then arrange the skewers on a large, flat plate. Cover with vented plastic wrap and microwave on full power until cooked the way you like it, about 5½ minutes for medium rare (rearrange the skewers a couple of times during microwaving, so they'll cook evenly). Let stand for about 2 minutes.

Meanwhile, scoop the extra sauce (you'll have about 1 Tbs or 15 ml) into a small dish and add 2 Tbs (30 ml) of water and stir to combine. You may also add more hot pepper sauce if you like. Then cover with vented plastic wrap and microwave on full power until heated through, about 30 seconds. Serve with skewered beef.

Browning Dish Note: Follow manufacturer's instructions, or preheat a nonstick browning dish for about 6 minutes. Arrange 3 to 4 skewers on the dish and microwave, uncovered, on full power (rearranging and flipping every minute) until done the way you like them, about 3 minutes for medium rare. Repeat with the rest of the skewers.

Garlic Chili (*Harissa*) Sauce

This sauce is famous in North Africa and it's perfect for roasted and skewered meats. Thanks to the microwave, the amount of oil can be greatly reduced.

Makes about ½ cup • 257 calories per recipe

6	dried chili peppers, seeds removed	
6	cloves garlic	
1	bay leaf	
	water or chicken stock to cover	
1 Tbs	olive oil	15 ml
⅓ cup	chicken stock	80 ml
2 Tbs	cider vinegar	30 ml

In a small dish combine the chilies, garlic, bay leaf and water or stock. Cover with vented plastic wrap and microwave on full power until the chilies are soft and tender, about 10 minutes. Check midway and add more water if necessary. Also, open a window because the chili fumes can be strong and irritating to the eyes and nose. Let the chilies stand for 10 minutes. Remove bay leaf.

Scoop the softened chilies into a processor or blender and whiz, adding the oil, stock and vinegar while the motor is running. You'll end up with a smooth paste that's a lively sauce for meats.

Mustard Sauce

A great condiment for hot and chilled meats and a great break from calorie-laden sauces.

Makes about ½ cup • 79 calories per recipe

½ cup	buttermilk	120 ml
1 tsp	cornstarch	5 ml
pinch	cream of tartar	
2 tsp	Dijon-style mustard	10 ml
1 Tbs	very finely minced fresh parsley or chives	15 ml
splash	Worcestershire sauce	

In a small bowl whisk together the buttermilk, cornstarch and cream of tartar. Microwave uncovered on full power until it begins to thicken, 1½ to 2 minutes, stirring a couple of times. Next, whisk in the mustard, parsley or chives and Worcestershire. Chill before serving.

Microwaving Reduces Fat and Calories

The June 1984 issue of the *Journal of the American Dietetic Association* published a report that announced microwaving as the leanest way to cook ground beef patties. Cooking methods compared were electric broiling, charbroiling, roasting, convection heating, frying and microwaving. Patties from ground round, ground chuck and regular ground beef were cooked and, in comparison with other methods, microwaving always produced patties containing the least fat and calories.

BEEF WITH GARLIC SAUCE

Serve on nests of sprouts and sliced asparagus, or over rice. It's also a good main-dish salad when sprinkled with toasted pine nuts and served with romaine or endive petals. Chilled papaya slices make a refreshing dessert with this dish.

4 servings • 179 calories per serving

3 Tbs	*nam pla** or 2 Tbs (30 ml) light soy sauce	45 ml
2 Tbs	freshly squeezed lemon juice	30 ml
2	cloves garlic, mashed to a paste	
1 lb	lean top round, sirloin or fillet, thinly sliced against the grain	450 g
	coarsely chopped scallions for tossing	
	firm, flavorful tomato wedges for tossing	
	watercress or arugula leaves for tossing	

Combine the *nam pla* or soy sauce, lemon juice and garlic in a 9-inch (23-cm) glass pie dish. Then add the beef to the garlic sauce. Let marinate for at least 2 hours.

Spread the beef out in the dish, cover with vented plastic wrap and microwave on full power until cooked the way you like it, about 5 minutes for medium rare (stir the beef a couple of times during microwaving). Let stand for 2 minutes and toss with scallions, tomatoes and watercress or arugula leaves before serving.

Browning Dish Note: Follow manufacturer's instructions, or preheat a nonstick browning dish for about 4 minutes. Spread half the beef out on the dish and microwave, uncovered, on full power (flipping every minute) until done the way you like it, 2½ to 3 minutes for medium rare. Repeat with the rest of the beef.

*Nam pla is a dark, flavorful and pungent, fish-based sauce that's available at Oriental markets and specialty foods stores.

SLICED BEEF SALAD WITH POTATO BATONS

Serve on shredded greens with crusty Italian bread on the side.

4 servings • 213 calories per serving

⅓ cup	fresh basil leaves	80 ml
1 tsp	grated lemon peel	5 ml
2	cloves garlic, peeled	
1 tsp	olive oil	5 ml
1 lb	lean sirloin, sliced into thin strips	450 g
½ lb	waxy-type potatoes	225 g
	freshly grated Parmesan for sprinkling	
	chopped pecans for sprinkling	

Combine the basil, lemon peel, garlic and oil in a processor or blender and whiz until you have a paste. Then toss the beef strips well with the paste. Let the mixture marinate for at least an hour.

Meanwhile, slice the potatoes into 3- × ½-inch (8- × 1-cm) bâtons. Tip them into a small dish with a splash of water, cover with vented plastic wrap and microwave on full power until tender, 2 to 2½ minutes.

When you're ready to eat, scoop the meat, marinade too, into a 9-inch (23-cm) glass pie dish and cover with vented plastic wrap. Microwave on full power until cooked the way you like it, about 5 minutes for medium rare (stir the meat a couple of times during microwaving). Immediately toss with potatoes and sprin-

kle with Parmesan and pecans. Then let stand for about 2 minutes before serving.

Browning Dish Note: Follow manufacturer's instructions, or preheat a nonstick browning dish for about 5 minutes. Spread the meat (reserve marinade) out on the dish and microwave uncovered on full power (flipping every minute) until done the way you like it, about 2½ minutes for medium rare.

Before you assemble the salad, pour the marinade into a small dish, cover and microwave on full power until heated through, about 1½ minutes.

Venison Sauce

Use with spaghetti, ravioli, lasagna or drizzled over corn bread or omelettes.

4 servings • 163 calories per serving

1 lb	ground venison	450 g
1½ cups	tomato puree	360 ml
2 Tbs	red wine vinegar	30 ml
⅓ cup	finely minced carrots	80 ml
⅓ cup	finely minced onions	80 ml
⅓ cup	finely minced celery	80 ml
2	cloves garlic, finely minced	
½ tsp	basil	2 ml
½ tsp	thyme	2 ml
½ tsp	oregano	2 ml

Spread the venison out in a 9-inch (23-cm) glass pie dish and cover with vented plastic wrap. Microwave on full power until just about cooked through, 4½ to 5 minutes. Drain if necessary, but venison is generally lean and there probably won't be much fat.

Next, add the rest of the ingredients to the venison in the same dish, combine well and microwave, uncovered, on full power until fragrant, bubbly and slightly thick, 7 to 8 minutes (stir a couple of times during microwaving). Let stand for about 3 minutes before serving.

Variation: Use lean ground beef instead of venison and note that it will probably need draining.

Savannah Barbecue Sauce

This is a thin, tangy sauce that should be used only for basting during the last 5 minutes of grilling or the meat could burn. It's similar to one served at a terrific barbecue restaurant in Savannah, Georgia, except this version omits salt and instead employs several other tangy flavorings.

Makes about 1 cup • 189 calories per recipe

½ cup	tomato puree	120 ml
¼ cup	cider vinegar	60 ml
1 Tbs	Worcestershire sauce	15 ml
½ tsp	hot pepper sauce, or to taste	2 ml
2	cloves garlic, mashed	
2 tsp	sweet butter	10 ml
1	bay leaf	
pinch	ground ginger	

In a small bowl combine all of the ingredients and cover with vented plastic wrap. Microwave on full power until fragrant and just bubbly, about 2 minutes. Let stand for about 5 minutes. Remove bay leaf before using.

You may make this sauce ahead and refrigerate until needed.

GREEK MEATBALLS (KEFTEDES)

Serve with a salad of zucchini chunks, ripe tomatoes, minced fresh mint, a splash of olive oil and crumbled feta cheese.

4 servings • 357 calories per serving

1 lb	lean ground beef or lamb	450 g
1	egg, beaten	
¼ cup	finely minced onions	60 ml
2 Tbs	bread crumbs	30 ml
1	clove garlic, finely minced	
1 tsp	oregano	5 ml
1 Tbs	minced fresh mint	15 ml
1 Tbs	freshly squeezed lemon juice	15 ml
½ cup	thick, plain, low-fat yogurt (drain to thicken)	120 ml
	fresh mint sprigs for garnishing	

In a large bowl combine the beef or lamb, egg, onions, bread crumbs, garlic, oregano, mint and lemon juice and mix well (using your hands is the best way). Next, form the mixture into walnut-size meatballs. You'll have about 40.

Set 15 meatballs at a time in a circle on a large, flat plate, cover with vented plastic wrap and microwave on full power until cooked through, about 3 minutes.

Meanwhile, scoop the yogurt into a large, wide dish and as the meatballs come out of the microwave, drain them if necessary and tip them into the yogurt. Let stand for 5 minutes, then garnish with the mint sprigs and serve.

BEEF
WITH WINTER
VEGETABLES

The herbs and flavorings combine to give full, rich flavors without the addition of salt. Serve over wide noodles tossed with poppy seeds.

4 servings • 179 calories per serving

¾ lb	lean top round, thinly sliced against the grain	340 g
1	carrot, finely minced	
1	parsnip, finely minced	
¼ cup	finely minced rutabagas	60 ml
2	bay leaves	
½ tsp	thyme	2 ml
1 Tbs	olive oil	15 ml
1 Tbs	balsamic vinegar or red wine vinegar	15 ml
¼ cup	tomato puree	60 ml
	minced fresh parsley for sprinkling	
	freshly ground black pepper for sprinkling	

Horseradish Cream

Spread on bread for roast beef sandwiches or serve with sliced hot or cold meats.

Makes about ½ cup • 99 calories per recipe

½ cup	milk or light cream	120 ml
1 tsp	cornstarch	5 ml
pinch	cream of tartar	
1 Tbs	prepared horseradish	15 ml
1 tsp	very finely minced fresh parsley or chives	5 ml

In a small bowl whisk together the milk or cream, cornstarch and cream of tartar. Set the bowl on a plate in case the sauce boils over a bit, then microwave, uncovered, until the sauce begins to thicken, 3 to 3½ minutes, stirring 2 or 3 times during microwaving. Next whisk in the horseradish and parsley and chill before serving.

In a 9-inch (23-cm) glass pie dish combine the beef, carrots, parsnips, rutabagas, bay leaves, thyme, oil, vinegar and puree. Cover and let marinate, refrigerated, overnight. If you can, let it come to room temperature before microwaving. Then cover with vented plastic wrap and microwave on full power until the beef is done the way you like it, about 5 minutes for medium rare. Sprinkle with parsley and pepper and let stand for about 3 minutes. Remove bay leaves and serve.

LOUISIANA BROIL WITH CAJUN HOT SAUCE

Of course, your microwave won't broil, but if you use it to marinate the meat you can save time and calories. Instead of marinating overnight in the refrigerator, the meat is microwaved on a low power for several minutes. And no fat is needed in the marinade because the microwave keeps the meat moist.

4 servings • 184 calories per serving

1 lb	lean top round or sirloin		450 g
2	medium tomatoes, chopped		
½ tsp	hot pepper sauce, or to taste		2 ml
2 Tbs	finely minced onions		30 ml
½ tsp	finely minced celery leaves		2 ml
½ tsp	thyme		2 ml
5	black peppercorns, finely ground		
5	white peppercorns, finely ground		

Set the meat in a 9-inch (23-cm) glass pie dish. Then, in a medium bowl combine the tomatoes, hot pepper sauce, onions, celery, thyme and peppercorns and pour it over the meat, rubbing on all sides with your hands. Cover with vented plastic wrap and microwave on medium-low power for about 4 minutes, flipping the meat midway.

Broil the meat for about half the normal time, on each side. In other words, if the meat is about an inch (2.5-cm) thick, you'd normally broil it for about 5 minutes on each side for medium rare. Now you'd broil it for about 2½ minutes per side. Meanwhile, microwave the remaining marinade, uncovered, on full power until most of the liquid has evaporated, about 2 minutes. Serve as a condiment for the meat.

ST. JOE RIBS
IN A BAG

St. Joseph, Missouri, is not, for the most part, a hotbed of culinary fascination. But it does produce some of the sweetest and most delicious pork imaginable. Here's a lean tribute to St. Joe.

4 servings • 71 calories per serving

2 lb	country pork ribs (2 pieces, trimmed of fat and halved)	1 kg
1½ cups	tomato puree	360 ml
	juice of 1 lemon	
3 Tbs	Worcestershire sauce	45 ml
2	cloves garlic, finely minced	
1	onion, chunked	
3	bay leaves	

Set the ribs on a roasting rack with a dish underneath to catch any remaining fat. Cover all with vented plastic wrap and microwave on full power for about 7 minutes, rotating and flipping the ribs twice. This procedure will rid the ribs of lots of fat and it's a good pre-grilling trick to remember.

Next set an oven cooking bag in a support dish and add in the ribs. Stir together the tomato puree, lemon juice, Worcestershire, garlic, onions and bay leaves and pour the sauce over the ribs. Seal the bag by tying a knot near the top (do not use the tie that comes with it) and use a knife to make a few slits in it. Microwave on full power until cooked through, about 15 minutes, rotating the dish twice. Then refrigerate in the bag for at least 3 hours, but overnight is best. This allows the flavors to become acquainted. When you're ready to eat, you can microwave, directly from the refrigerator, on full power until heated through, 3 to 4 minutes. Remove bay leaves and serve.

TOURNEDOS OF BEEF WITH GARLIC-JALAPEÑO PUREE

One popular way of enjoying beef is by poaching. Unlike boiling beef, poaching is gentler and more flavorful. And unlike sautéing and broiling, when beef is poached no fat is needed to keep it juicy.

4 servings • 348 calories per serving

7	cloves garlic, peeled	
⅓ cup	beef stock	80 ml
1	bay leaf	
1	jalapeño pepper, seeded and coarsely chopped (wear plastic gloves when handling)	
4	tournedos of beef (about 3 oz or 85 g each), sliced horizontally to make thin disks	
	more beef stock to cover	
3	bay leaves	
¼ cup	buttermilk	60 ml
	chive blossoms or watercress sprigs for garnishing	

Combine the garlic, stock, bay leaf and jalapeños in a small bowl. Cover with vented plastic wrap and microwave on full power until the garlic is fragrant and tender to the touch, about 5 minutes. Check from time to time to make sure the stock hasn't boiled away. If it has, add a bit more. Let it stand while you prepare the meat.

Set the tournedo halves in a 9-inch (23-cm) glass pie dish with stock to cover and the bay leaves. Cover with vented plastic wrap and microwave on full power until done the way you like, about 4 minutes for medium rare. If the stock is cold your microwaving time will increase. Let the tournedos stand while you finish preparing the puree.

Scoop the garlic mixture (with bay leaf removed) into a processor or blender and whiz until smooth, trickling in the buttermilk while the motor is running.

(continued)

To serve, pour a pool of puree on each of 4 hot serving plates and set 2 drained tournedo disks (with bay leaves removed) on each pool. Chive blossoms or watercress sprigs are nice garnishes but you may use whatever green sprigs you have around.

Browning Dish Note: Follow manufacturer's instructions, or preheat a nonstick browning dish for about 4 minutes. Arrange the disks on the dish (eliminate the poaching stock and bay leaves) and microwave, uncovered, on full power (flipping midway) until done the way you like, about 2 minutes for medium rare.

Aromatics for Meats

Here are some wonderful ideas for using your microwave to jazz up meats without salt or fat.

Sichuan peppercorns, also called *fagara,* are not really peppercorns, but try telling that to your mouth after you've eaten some. Normally they're roasted, usually in oil, to release their fragrance. By microwaving you can do the same without the oil. Here's how: Pour 1 teaspoon (5 ml) of sichuan peppercorns into a small bowl and microwave, uncovered, until fragrant, 1 to 2 minutes, then grind in a mortar. Their spicy, earthy aroma is wonderful in a marinade for beef or pork along with some soy sauce, stock, garlic and dry sherry. You can also mix the ground peppercorns with a bit of mustard and rub into a pork or beef roast before roasting. When ground very fine, you can combine the peppercorns with soy sauce, stock and a splash of chili oil and use as a dipping sauce for sliced meats.

Mignonette is also called shot pepper. Its most famous use is in steak *au poivre*. The microwave does a good job of warming the pepper without the customary salt and fat. Combine 1 teaspoon (5 ml) each of black and white peppercorns in a small dish and microwave, uncovered, until fragrant, about 2 minutes. Then crack the pepper so it's not crushed but still in pieces. It's delicious rubbed into noisettes of lamb before sautéing or grilling.

Cumin seed is often used with meats in the cuisines of Mexico and India. When a recipe suggests heating the seeds in fat to release their flavors, microwave instead. One teaspoon (5 ml) will take about 2 minutes, uncovered, on full power. Let stand for 2 minutes before proceeding with the recipe.

MARINATED STUFFED BEEF (MATAMBRE)

Matambre *(mah-TOM-bray) is a specialty from South America. Thin sheets of beef are marinated, then filled with vegetable julienne, rolled, cooked and sliced into disks for serving. In this version no fat is needed to keep the beef sheets moist because the microwave won't dry them out.*

4 servings • 141 calories per serving

⅔ lb	lean top round	300 g
2 tsp	Worcestershire sauce	10 ml
2	cloves garlic, mashed	
2 Tbs	beef stock	30 ml
1	small carrot, cut into fine julienne	
1	small zucchini, cut into fine julienne	
1	sweet red pepper, cut into fine julienne	
½ tsp	oregano	2 ml
½ tsp	thyme	2 ml

Have the butcher slice the beef into very thin sheets, no thicker than ¼ inch (.5 cm). Ideally you'll have 4 sheets (9 × 5 inches or 23 × 12 cm each). Arrange the sheets in a large baking pan and add in the Worcestershire, garlic and stock, rubbing them into the meat with your hands. Let the sheets marinate for about 30 minutes.

To assemble the *matambre,* lay a sheet of beef out in front of you, horizontally. Arrange a quarter of the carrot, zucchini and pepper strips in a tidy pile clear across half of the sheet that's closest to you. Sprinkle on a pinch of oregano and thyme. Roll up jelly roll style and tie in 2 places with string. Repeat with the remaining sheets. Then roll each in the remaining marinade.

Set the rolls on the edges of a large dinner plate, cover with vented plastic wrap and microwave on full power until cooked through, about 5 minutes, flipping the rolls over midway. Let stand for about 5 minutes. If you like, run them under the broiler briefly to glaze them with color. Slice into disks and serve, discarding string.

Note: If you have extra beef stock and Worcestershire, combine them to taste and serve as a dipping sauce with the *matambre.* Horseradish Cream (page 179) is also a very delicious accompaniment.

VEAL WITH DRIED TOMATOES AND MOZZARELLA

Microwaving is an excellent cooking method for veal. It requires little fat yet keeps the meat moist and tender. Now, here's the trick: The veal must be uniform in thickness, color and texture or it won't cook evenly.

4 servings • 271 calories per serving (not including linguine)

8	dried tomatoes, minced	
2 Tbs	chicken stock	30 ml
1 lb	veal scallopini, cut into very thin, uniform strips	450 g
2 Tbs	freshly squeezed lemon juice	30 ml
2 tsp	olive oil	10 ml
⅓ cup	grated mozzarella	80 ml
2 Tbs	minced fresh parsley	30 ml
½ lb	cooked hot linguine	225 g

Combine the tomatoes and stock in a small bowl and cover with vented plastic wrap. Microwave on full power until the tomatoes are tender, 3 to 4 minutes. Let them stand while you prepare the veal.

Arrange the veal in a 9-inch (23-cm) glass pie dish and toss with the lemon juice and oil. Cover with vented plastic wrap and microwave on full power until cooked through, 4 to 4½ minutes.

Immediately add the tomatoes and their liquid, mozzarella and parsley and let stand until the mozzarella has melted, about 4 minutes. Toss with linguine and serve.

VEAL WITH CITRUS AND SAGE

4 servings • 183 calories per serving

Combine the veal, lemon and lime juices, honey and sage in a 9-inch (23-cm) glass pie dish and arrange the lemon and lime slices over it. Cover with vented plastic wrap and microwave on full power until the veal is cooked through, about 4½ minutes. Let stand for 2 minutes. Discard the citrus slices.

Note: The veal is delicious with a side of steaming asparagus spears.

1 lb	veal scallopini, cut into very thin, uniform pieces	450 g
2 Tbs	freshly squeezed lemon juice	30 ml
2 Tbs	freshly squeezed lime juice	30 ml
1 tsp	honey	5 ml
½ tsp	sage	2 ml
½	lemon, thinly sliced	
½	lime, thinly sliced	

Tangy Fruit Glaze

Here's a glaze with no added salt, fat or refined sugar. Try painting it on roasts of pork, lamb, or beef or spare ribs before roasting.

4 servings • 42 calories per serving

1 cup	unsweetened pineapple juice	240 ml
1 Tbs	Dijon-style mustard	15 ml
2 tsp	cornstarch	10 ml
¼ tsp	tamarind paste or concentrate*	1 ml
pinch	cream of tartar	

Whisk together all of the ingredients in a 9-inch (23-cm) glass pie dish. Don't worry if the tamarind doesn't dissolve in this sauce right away. It will eventually. Microwave, uncovered, on full power until thickened and bubbly, 7 to 8 minutes stirring every 2 minutes.

*Tamarind comes from tropical tamarind pods and tastes like a combination of molasses and lemon. It's available at Oriental markets, East Indian markets and specialty foods stores.

SOFT TORTILLAS WITH PICCADILLO *FILLING*

Serve with corn on the cob and sliced ripe tomatoes.

4 servings • 301 calories per serving

½ lb	lean ground beef	225 g
1	small apple, peeled and grated	
2	tomatoes, juiced and chopped	
1	jalapeño pepper, seeded and minced (wear plastic gloves when handling)	
2	cloves garlic, minced	
2 Tbs	raisins, minced	30 ml
½ tsp	oregano	2 ml
pinch	ground cumin	
pinch	ground coriander	
pinch	ground cinnamon	
4	large, soft flour tortillas shredded Monterey Jack cheese for sprinkling	

In a 9-inch (23-cm) glass pie dish combine the beef, apples, tomatoes, jalapeños, garlic, raisins, oregano, cumin, coriander and cinnamon and cover with vented plastic wrap. Microwave on full power until the beef is cooked through and the mixture begins to look like a thick sauce, about 10 minutes (stir or shake a couple of times during microwaving). Let the *piccadillo* stand for about 3 minutes, then scoop about ½ cup (120 ml) in a log shape onto each tortilla, fold in the sides and roll. Set them seam side down in the same dish and sprinkle with the cheese. Cover with vented plastic wrap and microwave on medium power until the cheese has melted, about 2 minutes.

LAMB WITH GARLIC AND LEMON

4 servings • 245 calories per serving

1 lb	lamb, trimmed of fat and sliced into thin ribbons	450 g
1	lemon, thinly sliced	
2	cloves garlic, thinly sliced	
1 tsp	olive oil	5 ml
	shredded spinach for tossing	

Tip lamb into a 9-inch (23-cm) glass pie dish and add the lemon slices, garlic and oil and toss to combine. Cover with vented plastic wrap and microwave on full power until cooked the way you like it, about 5 minutes for medium rare, stirring midway. Toss with the spinach and let stand for 4 minutes before serving.

Variation: Toss with rice and serve at room temperature or chilled as a main-dish salad.

Browning Dish Note: Follow manufacturer's instructions, or preheat a nonstick browning dish for about 4 minutes. Spread the lamb (lemon, garlic and oil included) out on the dish and microwave, uncovered, on full power (flipping every minute) until done the way you like it, about 2½ minutes for medium rare. Don't burn the garlic or it could become bitter.

ENLIGHTENED ENTRÉES

Some very good friends, who are about to be very surprised ones, frequently help me evaluate my newly created recipes. They don't always know where the recipes will be published. But that's really not what matters. Their job is to judge if the food is delicious and enjoyable. For instance, if I've baked breads for a magazine article on high-fiber foods, the high-fiber part is secondary. What really matters is whether or not the bread is good. After all, if it's heavy and tasteless, it doesn't matter how healthy it is because nobody's going to want to eat it.

Well, these good folks have eaten their way through this book with enthusiasm. And after each tasting, one or the other of them has said, "Just don't start feeding us any microwave stuff." I never said anything. I'm delighted to know that the food in this book is not just "good for microwaved food," but good food period.

I'm particularly pleased with the offerings in this chapter because they're vegetarian, but neither strange nor boring. They're delicious, imaginative and light. In other words, enlightened. Consider Eggplant Steaks with Black Bean Sauce, Jalapeño Crepes with Hominy and Avocado, Pumpkin Gnocchi with Sweet Butter and Parmesan—not exactly entrées to shove on the back burner.

Many of these entrées can also be used as side dishes or parts of buffets. Spaghetti Squash with Golden

Bread Crumbs, for example, can be served as an entrée with crisp greens and a cup of steaming soup, or as a side dish with poached fish or grilled chicken. It also, as most of the other pastas, can become a tasty main dish salad when served room temperature on romaine petals. It all depends on your imagination.

CRISP TORTILLAS WITH BLACK BEANS AND YAMS

4 servings • 268 calories per serving

Tip the yams into a 9-inch (23-cm) glass pie dish along with the garlic and water or stock. Cover with vented plastic wrap and microwave on full power until tender, about 3 minutes. Let stand for 2 minutes, then drain if necessary.

In a processor or blender combine the yam mixture, beans, oregano, curry powder, pepper flakes and butter and whiz until smooth and combined. Scoop into taco shells, garnish with tomatoes, scallions and onions and serve.

Note: If you'd rather, use flour tortillas or crepes instead of taco shells. The mixture is also delicious stuffed into cooked acorn squash or used in omelettes.

1	yam (about ¾ lb or 340 g), peeled and chopped	
2	cloves garlic, smashed	
1 Tbs	water or chicken stock	15 ml
2 cups	cooked black beans	480 ml
1 tsp	oregano	5 ml
pinch	curry powder	
¼ tsp	dried red pepper flakes	1 ml
1 Tbs	sweet butter	15 ml
4	taco shells	
	chopped ripe tomatoes for garnishing	
	minced scallions for garnishing	
	minced purple onions for garnishing	

VEGETABLE FRITTATA ARLES

The colors in this frittata may remind you of some of van Gogh's paintings of gardens in Arles, France. Serve it for lunch or light dinner with crisp greens and steaming redskins.

When microwaving frittatas and omelettes never add salt because it can reduce fluffiness, plus it promotes uneven cooking because the little grains attract microwaves. Also, make sure the eggs are well beaten because if they're not, they'll cook unevenly and leave tough streaks.

4 servings • 82 calories per serving

2 Tbs	minced carrots		30 ml
¼ cup	minced broccoli		60 ml
1	scallion, finely minced		
2 Tbs	grated Gruyère cheese		30 ml
3	eggs		
2 Tbs	milk		30 ml
	freshly ground black pepper for sprinkling		

Spray a 9-inch (23-cm) glass pie dish with vegetable cooking spray and toss in the carrots, broccoli, scallions and Gruyère. Beat the eggs with the milk and pour over the vegetables and Gruyère. Cover with vented plastic wrap and microwave on medium power until the eggs are set, 6 to 7 minutes, rotating the dish a couple of times during cooking. Let stand 4 minutes. Sprinkle with freshly ground black pepper and serve warm in wedges.

Variation: Replace the carrots and broccoli with minced fresh spinach and corn kernels.

JALAPEÑO CREPES WITH HOMINY AND AVOCADO

Unlike crepes done on the stove top, these need no butter or fat to keep them from sticking. Plus, unlike many microwaved crepes, they're soft and tender. One secret to tenderness is making sure the eggs and milk are room temperature before you begin. Serve with a ripe tomato salad.

4 servings • 227 calories per serving

2	eggs, room temperature	
¼ cup	milk, warmed in microwave	60 ml
1	jalapeño pepper, seeded and minced (wear plastic gloves when handling)	
2 Tbs	minced sweet red peppers	30 ml
1 Tbs	whole wheat pastry flour	15 ml
½ tsp	oregano	2 ml
⅔ cup	cooked hominy or corn kernels	160 ml
1	avocado, peeled, seeded and chopped	
½ cup	grated Monterey Jack cheese	120 ml

In a small bowl whisk together the eggs, milk, peppers, flour and oregano. Spray a 9-inch (23-cm) glass pie dish with vegetable cooking spray and pour in 3 Tbs (45 ml) of batter. Tip the batter around until it's a 5- to 6-inch (12- to 15-cm) round crepe. Microwave, uncovered, on medium power until the crepe is cooked, about 2 minutes and 40 seconds. Flip the crepe out face side down onto waxed paper and repeat the process with the remaining batter, spraying the dish each time. You'll have 4 crepes.

Arrange the hominy or corn kernels, avocado and half the cheese in log shapes on one side of each crepe. Then roll up.

Set each crepe seam side down on the same dish and sprinkle the remaining cheese over them. Microwave, uncovered, on medium power until the cheese is melted, about 1 minute. Serve warm.

More Ideas for Using Crepes

Omit the jalapeño and sweet red peppers from the batter, then:

• Stuff with ricotta and top with tomato sauce and grated mozzarella. Microwave on medium power until heated through and the cheese is melted.

- Add snipped fresh dill to the crepe batter and wrap a poached egg in each finished crepe. Serve with tangy mustard and smoked salmon.
- Fill with cooked broccoli florets and toasted peanuts. Serve with a dipping sauce of stock and a splash each of soy sauce and toasted sesame oil.
- Fill with fresh chevre that's been mixed with minced fresh basil and thyme. Serve with fresh pears.

Savory Mexican Pie *(Chilaquiles)*

My brother and I always called this dish Ten-Layer Mexican Stuff. Then we found out it had a name—chilaquiles (Chila-KEE-lase). Imagine my surprise when I discovered that the concept had existed for years and actually had an official name. Whatever you call it, it's a lot of fun to eat and is especially delicious with a side of cooked zucchini coins and some extra tortillas.

4 to 6 servings

The idea is to layer the ingredients in a 9-inch (23-cm) glass pie dish. And don't feel tied to the ingredients suggested here, use what you're in the mood for. Sliced black olives and minced hot chilies are nice additions. Just remember that if you use meat, cook and drain it first to get rid of its fat. Here's a list of ingredients in order of their layering.

flour tortillas, torn to pieces
cooked pinto beans
chopped tomato
chopped sweet onion
cooked rice
chopped green chilies
minced fresh parsley or coriander
corn kernels
tomato salsa
shredded cheese for sprinkling

Use a small handful of each ingredient, or to taste. Cover with vented plastic wrap and microwave on full power until heated through, about 4 minutes. Immediately sprinkle with the cheese and let stand for about 4 minutes more. Slice like a pie (a gooey one) and serve.

STUFFED SWEET PEPPERS WITH FRESH TOMATO SAUCE

This stuffing is vegetarian but you may use any you like by following the recipe concept. If you add meat, cook it first to get rid of its fat.

4 servings • 125 calories per serving

Slice the tops off the sweet peppers and scoop out their insides with a spoon (mince the tops and save them for later). Wrap each pepper in waxed paper and microwave on full power until they just begin to get soft, about 3 minutes.

Meanwhile, in a small bowl combine the corn, rice, onions, chili powder, cumin, oregano, turmeric and orange peel. When the peppers are cool enough to handle, stuff them with the mixture. Then set the peppers in a large, casserole-type dish, cover and microwave on full power until cooked through, about 5 minutes. Immediately uncover and sprinkle with cheese. Then let stand while you prepare the sauce.

4	medium sweet peppers, red, yellow or green	
¾ cup	corn kernels	180 ml
¾ cup	cooked rice	180 ml
1 Tbs	finely minced sweet onions	15 ml
¼ tsp	hot, Mexican-type chili powder	1 ml
½ tsp	cumin seeds, ground	2 ml
1 tsp	oregano	5 ml
pinch	turmeric	
pinch	freshly grated orange peel	
	grated sharp cheddar for sprinkling	
2	ripe medium tomatoes	
1 Tbs	minced fresh parsley	15 ml
1 tsp	minced jalapeño pepper (wear plastic gloves when handling)	5 ml

Combine the tomatoes, parsley, jalapeños and pepper tops in a blender or processor and whiz until combined. Serve with the peppers.

CORN CAKE WITH RICOTTA AND PIMIENTOS

Although similar to a polenta you'd find in the north of Italy, this one takes quite a bit less time and devotion.

4 servings • 243 calories per serving

¾ cup	yellow cornmeal	180 ml
¾ cup	chicken stock	180 ml
¾ cup	plain, low-fat yogurt	180 ml
2	eggs, beaten	
⅔ cup	corn kernels	160 ml
1¼ tsp	baking powder	6 ml
½ tsp	oregano	2 ml
¼ tsp	thyme	1 ml
½ cup	part-skim ricotta	120 ml
2	pimientos, thinly sliced	

Spray a 9-inch (23-cm) glass pie dish with vegetable cooking spray. Then in a medium bowl whisk together the cornmeal, stock, yogurt, eggs, corn kernels, baking powder, oregano and thyme. Pour into the dish, cover with vented plastic wrap and microwave on full power for 2 minutes. Uncover and stir immediately. Then cover and continue to microwave on full power until the center is firm to the touch, about 6 more minutes. Let stand, uncovered, for 10 minutes. Slice into wedges, top each with ricotta and pimientos and serve warm.

Note: If you like, you can sauté each wedge in a bit of sweet butter for a couple of minutes on each side, before topping and serving. This is especially nice for leftover wedges.

Basil for Pesto

If you've ever needed fresh basil and been stuck with only dried, here's how your microwave can help. Measure 3 tablespoons (45 ml) of dried basil into a small dish with sides. Pour in ¼ cup (60 ml) of water, cover with vented plastic wrap and microwave on full power until the water is completely absorbed and the basil is fragrant, about 3 minutes. You'll have about ¼ cup (60 ml) of chopped basil to use for making pesto. Or combine it with ricotta and toss with hot pasta.

SWISS FONDUE (RACLETTE)

Serve, as the Swiss do, for dinner on chilly evenings. If you're watching your salt and cholesterol, use a Heidi-type Swiss cheese rather than the baby Swiss.

4 servings • 335 calories per serving

6 oz	shredded fontina cheese	170 g
6 oz	shredded baby Swiss cheese	170 g
2 Tbs	nonalcoholic dry white wine	30 ml
1 tsp	Worcestershire sauce	5 ml

Accompaniments
Cooked, baby new potatoes
crusty French bread
crisp, tart apple slices

Combine the cheeses, wine and Worcestershire in a 9-inch (23-cm) glass pie dish, cover with vented plastic wrap and microwave on medium power until the cheese has melted, 4 to 5 minutes. Uncover and stir very well midway.

At the table, diners scoop a pool of hot cheese onto their plates and enjoy with the accompaniments.

Ideas for Serving Poached Eggs

Poached eggs are probably among the first foods you tried in your microwave. They're easy and they're usually the first recipe to appear in the pamphlets that come with microwaves. Luckily, these simple treats can be jazzed up to create an exciting brunch, lunch or dinner. After poaching according to manufacturer's directions, serve them with:

- Grits, shredded spinach and red-eye gravy
- Chopped ripe tomatoes, fresh basil and shredded mozzarella
- Corn bread and sautéed sweet peppers
- Asparagus, tarragon-laced plain, low-fat yogurt and minced scallions
- Potato pancakes, sour cream and minced chives
- Sliced sautéed mushrooms and fresh thyme sprigs

ENCHILADAS WITH SWEET AND HOT CHILIES

Garnish with sliced avocado and serve with pinto beans and a spinach salad.

4 servings • 197 calories per serving

2 Tbs	chicken stock	30 ml
1 Tbs	olive oil	15 ml
4	scallions, finely minced	
2	cloves garlic, finely minced	
1	sweet red pepper, chopped	
1	mild green chili pepper, minced	
1	serrano chili pepper, minced	
2	tomatoes, juiced and chopped with juice reserved	
½ tsp	ground cumin	2 ml
½ tsp	ground coriander	2 ml
½ tsp	oregano	2 ml
½ tsp	Mexican-type chili powder	2 ml
10	drops hot pepper sauce, or to taste	
4	soft corn tortillas	
⅔ cup	grated Monterey Jack cheese	160 ml
¼ cup	reserved tomato juice	60 ml
1 tsp	Worcestershire sauce	5 ml

Make the filling by combining the stock, oil, scallions, garlic, peppers, chilies, tomatoes, cumin, coriander, oregano, chili powder and hot pepper sauce in a 9-inch (23-cm) glass pie dish. Cover with vented plastic wrap and microwave on full power until the tomatoes have wilted and the filling is thick, about 3 minutes. Stir or shake midway.

Then lay out the tortillas and sprinkle each with an equal amount of cheese, saving a bit for sprinkling later. Divide the filling among the tortillas, roll them and press in the filling on the sides with the back of a spoon.

Set the enchiladas seam side down into the same dish. Then combine the reserved tomato juice and Worcestershire in a small bowl and brush the enchiladas with the mixture. Cover with vented plastic wrap and microwave on medium power until heated through, about 4 minutes. Sprinkle with the remaining cheese and let stand until it's melted. Serve warm.

CHICK-PEA AND POTATO CURRY

Serve in flat bread, like pita, with mild white cheese. Or serve as an entrée salad, chilled, with plump grapes and bananas on the side. Make it ahead and the flavors will actually improve. You may use canned chick-peas but rinse them first to get rid of their salt.

4 servings • 163 calories per serving

2	potatoes (about 1 lb or 450 g), cubed	
1 cup	cooked chick-peas	240 ml
1	small onion, sliced	
½ cup	chopped spinach	120 ml
1 Tbs	chicken stock or water	15 ml
1 Tbs	peanut oil	15 ml
1 tsp	curry powder	5 ml
pinch	freshly grated nutmeg	
pinch	turmeric	
1 Tbs	dry white wine or nonalcoholic wine	15 ml
2 Tbs	tomato sauce	30 ml
1 Tbs	light cream or milk	15 ml

Combine the potatoes, chick-peas, onions, spinach and stock or water in a 9-inch (23-cm) glass pie dish and cover with vented plastic wrap. Microwave on full power until the potatoes are tender, 6 to 8 minutes, stirring or shaking midway. Drain if necessary and let stand while you prepare the curry.

Combine the oil, curry powder, nutmeg, turmeric, wine and tomato sauce in a small dish, cover with vented plastic wrap and microwave on full power until fragrant, 1 to 2 minutes. Pour over the potato mixture, add the cream or milk and toss well to combine.

Quick Cracked Wheat

Here's a chance to enjoy a wholesome, high-fiber grain in less time than ever before.

Makes about 2 cups • 151 calories per ½-cup serving

1 cup	coarse cracked wheat	240 ml
1½ cups	water	360 ml
1	bay leaf	

Combine the wheat, water and bay leaf in a 9-inch (23-cm) glass pie dish and cover with vented plastic wrap. Microwave on full power until the wheat is tender, 5 to 6 minutes. Let stand for 5 minutes. Remove bay leaf and if necessary, drain excess water before using.

Ideas for Using Cracked Wheat

- Toss with a vegetable curry and serve in a scooped-out pineapple half
- Toss with stir-fried Chinese vegetables and serve in lettuce petals
- Use to stuff peppers or eggplant
- Toss with tangerine sections, watercress, broccoli florets and lemon vinaigrette
- Toss with chopped apples, chopped celery, romaine, toasted walnuts and cider vinaigrette
- Toss with cherry tomatoes, sliced black olives, green beans, oregano-scented vinaigrette and crumbled feta
- Toss with tiny pasta, chopped artichoke hearts, fresh, flat-leaf parsley, shredded mozzarella and a clear vinaigrette
- Omit the bay leaf and enjoy for breakfast with vanilla yogurt and maple syrup
- For a creamy salad, toss still-hot cracked wheat with a bit of ricotta. Then stir in vegetables, fruits or herbs.

Pasta Tips

- To reheat 1 cup (240 ml) of sauced spaghetti or linguine, cover tightly with vented plastic wrap and microwave on full power until warmed through, about a minute. Sprinkle with freshly grated Parmesan and let stand for 1 minute before serving.
- Create a quick poppy seed sauce for pasta. First toast the seeds by pouring about 1 tablespoon (15 ml) into a dry 9-inch (23-cm) glass pie dish. Microwave, uncovered, at full power until fragrant, about 5 minutes. Then toss with a bit of sweet butter and hot pasta.

Tempting Tempeh

Tempeh is a little flat cake made of cultured soybeans and often some grains like rice and barley. It's famous in Indonesian cuisines and has a wonderful meaty texture and winey aroma. To microwave, cut the tempeh into equal-size chunks and toss with some stock and a splash of soy sauce. Add in some onion slices, ginger, minced garlic, slivered sweet peppers and a splash of chili oil. Cover with vented plastic wrap and microwave on full power. One-half pound (225 g) will take about 4 minutes. Sprinkle with minced chives and serve in romaine petals.

SPAGHETTI SQUASH

Here's the basic spaghetti squash procedure. It can be doubled but be sure to cook each half by itself to guarantee even cooking. Spaghetti Squash with Golden Bread Crumbs, which follows, is one idea for saucing, but tomato sauces and herbed cheese sauces are nice, too.

3½ lb	spaghetti squash, room temperature	2 kg

Halve the squash and scoop out the seeds. Set one half cut side down on wax paper and microwave on full power until the strands become loose and tender, 3½ to 4½ minutes. Let stand for 5 minutes and follow the procedure for the other half. When the squash is cool enough to handle, fluff out the strands with a fork.

SPAGHETTI SQUASH WITH GOLDEN BREAD CRUMBS

4 servings • 143 calories per serving

		strands from 1 cooked spaghetti squash (at left)	
1	Tbs	sweet butter	15 ml
1	Tbs	olive oil	15 ml
3	Tbs	dried bread crumbs	45 ml
1	Tbs	freshly grated Parmesan	15 ml
1	Tbs	minced fresh mint or parsley	15 ml

Arrange the strands in a large serving bowl and set it aside while you prepare the sauce.

Combine the butter and oil in a small dish and cover with vented plastic wrap. Microwave on full power until the butter has melted, about 1 minute. Stir in the bread crumbs, Parmesan and mint or parsley and toss with spaghetti squash strands.

SICHUAN NOODLES

Thin Chinese rice noodles are commonly soaked in water for 20 to 30 minutes before using. But when microwaved they take just a few minutes and their texture is not the least bit gummy. When handling rice noodles, and particularly when tossing with sauce, never stir. Instead, use tongs or fingers to lift and drop them. This will keep them from matting.

Serve Sichuan Noodles with clear consommé and broccoli that's been lightly cooked and tossed with a splash of sesame oil. The noodles are also nice served in lettuce petals and eaten as a finger food.

4 oz	thin rice noodles	110 g
2	slices fresh ginger	
1 Tbs	light soy sauce	15 ml
3 Tbs	peanut butter	45 ml
1 tsp	red wine vinegar	5 ml
1 Tbs	*mirin**	15 ml
1 Tbs	honey	15 ml
¼ tsp	hot pepper sauce, or to taste	1 ml
2 Tbs	chicken stock	30 ml
2 tsp	sesame oil	10 ml
splash	chili oil	
1 cup	thin green beans, sliced vertically	240 ml
3 cups	mung bean sprouts	720 ml
3	scallions, minced	

4 servings • 262 calories per serving

Set the noodles in a 9-inch (23-cm) glass pie dish and pour in enough water to cover. Add the ginger, cover with vented plastic wrap and microwave on full power until the noodles are tender, about 4 minutes, stirring midway. Drain the noodles, scoop them into a large bowl and let them stand while you prepare the sauce.

In the same dish combine the soy sauce, peanut butter, vinegar, *mirin,* honey, hot pepper sauce and stock. Cover with vented plastic wrap and microwave on full power until thick and fragrant, about 2 minutes. Pour over the noodles and use tongs or fingers to combine. Don't stir. Add the oils, beans, sprouts and scallions and continue to combine. Serve warm or room temperature.

*Available at Oriental markets.

CABBAGE BUNDLES

Please don't overcook cabbage until the poor, weary leaves are pleading for mercy. Instead, follow this procedure and enjoy them tender, crisp and green.

1	head cabbage

To prepare the leaves, use a knife to remove the core from a head of winter cabbage. Pull off any ugly outer leaves, then pull off 4 pretty ones and rinse them but don't dry. Stack the leaves together and wrap in plastic wrap. Then microwave on full power until the leaves are tender but still crisp, 3 to 4 minutes. Notice that the green of the leaves is enhanced. Let the leaves stand for about 5 minutes before stuffing, or make ahead and refrigerate.

You'll need about ½ cup (120 ml) of stuffing for each leaf. Here's an example of how all that works, including a stuffing recipe. Feel free to use your own stuffing, but if you're using meat, cook it first to get rid of its fat. If you're using cheese, microwave on medium power to prevent the cheese from becoming rubbery.

BROCCOLI RABE STUFFING FOR CABBAGE BUNDLES

4 servings • 125 calories per serving

1 tsp	sweet butter	5 ml
1 cup	chopped broccoli rabe, kale or spinach	240 ml
2 Tbs	minced onions	30 ml
½ cup	mashed cooked pinto beans	120 ml
1 cup	cooked rice	240 ml
4	cooked cabbage leaves (at left)	
¼ cup	chicken stock	60 ml

Combine the butter, broccoli rabe, kale or spinach and onions in a 9-inch (23-cm) glass pie dish, cover with vented plastic wrap and microwave on full power until the broccoli rabe, kale or spinach has wilted, 2½ to 3 minutes. Scoop the mixture into a medium bowl and stir in the beans and rice.

To stuff, snip out the stem part of each cabbage leaf, set about ½ cup (120 ml) of stuffing at the tip of each leaf, fold the sides in and roll up. Set the bundles, seam side down, in the same dish, pour the stock over them, cover with vented plastic wrap and microwave on full power until heated through, about 5 minutes. Let stand 3 minutes before serving.

SPAGHETTI TORTE WITH GARLIC AND PEPPERS

4 servings • 231 calories per serving

In a small dish combine the oil, garlic, thyme and bay leaf. Cover with vented plastic wrap and microwave on full power until fragrant, about 1½ minutes. Discard the bay leaf and scoop the oil, garlic and thyme into a large bowl. Add the chilies, peppers and spaghetti and mix well (using your hands is easiest). Then pour in the beaten eggs and continue to mix until all of the ingredients are coated.

Turn everything out into a lightly oiled 9-inch (23-cm) glass pie dish and press it down firmly. Cover with waxed paper and weight it with a round dinner plate. Microwave on full power until firm, 8 to

1	Tbs	olive oil	15 ml
	2	cloves garlic, thinly sliced	
½	tsp	thyme	2 ml
	1	bay leaf	
	2	mild green chili peppers, chopped	
	2	sweet red or green peppers, chopped	
3	cups	cooked spaghetti	720 ml
	2	eggs, beaten	
		freshly grated Parmesan for sprinkling	

10 minutes. Sprinkle with Parmesan and, if you like, run it under the broiler until just golden. To serve, cut into slices with kitchen shears.

STUFFED GRAPE LEAVES

This is nice picnic food that can be made ahead. The leaves are easy to prepare and can be filled with many wonderful stuffings. If you decide to use meat, cook it first to get rid of its fat.

16	fresh grape leaves

Rinse leaves and, without drying, stack and wrap loosely in plastic wrap. Microwave on full power until the leaves begin to be tender, 1 to 2 minutes, flipping the bundle midway. (If you're using jarred leaves, rinse them well in hot water to rid them of their salt, but don't microwave.)

Drain the leaves and lay them, shiny side down, with the stems facing you. If the stems and ribs are tough, cut them out. Next, place 1 to 2 Tbs (15 to 30 ml) of filling in the center of each leaf and fold the stem end over it. Fold in the sides and roll into little cigars.

Arrange the stuffed leaves in a 9-inch (23-cm) glass pie dish. Pour in ½ cup (120 ml) of chicken stock with a splash of lemon juice and cover with vented plastic wrap. Microwave on full power until heated through, about 10 minutes. Let stand for 10 minutes, drain and serve warm or chilled with a variety of mustards or tomato sauce for dipping.

Ideas for Stuffings

- Cooked rice, grated apples, dried currants, pine nuts and a pinch of thyme
- Cooked rice, chopped spinach, minced fresh scallions and minced fresh dill
- Cooked rice, chopped smoked salmon, minced chives and Dijon-style mustard
- Cooked rice, corn kernels, minced mild green chilies, minced serrano chilies and minced garlic. This one's tasty when microwaved in half non-alcoholic white wine and half chopped tomatoes.
- Cooked rice, minced cooked chicken, minced dried figs and minced fresh mint

Vegetable Frittata Arles (page 191)

Jalapeño Crepes with Hominy and Avocado (page 192)

Spaghetti Torte with Garlic and Peppers (page 203)

Pumpkin Seed Pesto (page 215)

Fruit Salad from Kariba (page 223)

Pear Fans in Mango Puree (page 227)

Glazed Fresh Peaches with Apricot Preserve (page 229)

Dessert Crepes (page 241)

BAMBOO PACKAGES FILLED WITH RICE

This is a rather exotic recipe, and although I hate to send you chasing after ingredients, the bamboo leaves are a must. They give a tealike perfume to the rice that's unlike any substitute. They're available at Oriental markets and are easy to spot. Look for long (18-inch or 45-cm), pale green bundles of about 50 dried leaves. By the way, this is quite a quantity but you can share them with a friend.

4 servings • 151 calories per serving

2 cups	cooked rice, like basmati	480 ml
2	medium carrots, finely minced	
2	scallions, minced	
1½ cups	minced cabbage	360 ml
1	clove garlic, minced	
¼ tsp	minced fresh ginger	1 ml
1 tsp	oyster sauce	5 ml
2 tsp	*mirin**	10 ml
1 tsp	sesame oil	5 ml
12	bamboo leaves	
1 cup	water	240 ml

In a large bowl combine the rice, carrots, scallions, cabbage, garlic, ginger, oyster sauce, *mirin* and oil.

Wet 3 bamboo leaves under running water. Set 2 parallel on a counter and overlap them an inch (2.5 cm) or two (5 cm) at their waistlines. Next scoop about a cup (240 ml) of the rice filling where the leaves overlap. Pull the bottom half of the leaves up over the filling and tuck them underneath it. Pull the top half of the leaves down over the package and tuck them under. Then slide the third leaf underneath the whole package and fold it up over the open sides. Make the package as tight as you can. Use string to tie the package like a little birthday gift and repeat, making 3 more packages.

Set the packages in a large glass baking dish and pour the water over them. Cover with vented plastic wrap and microwave on full power until cooked through and fragrant, about 10 minutes, flipping the packages over midway. Let stand for several minutes before letting each diner open his own. They're good cold, too.

Variation: If you can't locate bamboo leaves, use large kale or bok choy leaves and microwave the packages for 4½ to 5 minutes.

*Available at Oriental markets.

Six Super Pasta Sauces

It's true that most pasta is best cooked on top of the stove in lots of boiling, bubbling water. Enticing sauces, however, can be created in the microwave. Here are six super ones with serving suggestions included. Note that about ½ pound (225 g) of dry pasta is usually enough to feed four.

Watercress and Basil Sauce

Serve hot with thin, whole wheat spaghetti or in pasta salads with tiny shells, elbows or tubettini.

4 servings • 97 calories per serving

½ lb	watercress	225 g
½ cup	fresh basil	120 ml
2	shallots, minced	
1 Tbs	olive oil	15 ml
1 Tbs	sweet butter	15 ml
	crumbled blue cheese for tossing	

Discard the tough stems from the watercress and basil and rip them into very small pieces. Don't chop with a knife or in a processor because they could turn brown around the edges. Scoop the greens into a 9-inch (23-cm) glass pie dish and add the shallots, oil and butter. Cover with vented plastic wrap and microwave on full power until the greens have wilted, 1 to 2 minutes. Toss with pasta and crumbled blue cheese.

Broccoli and Ricotta Sauce

This is nice with spinach fettuccine or hay and straw, which is half spinach fettuccine and half white fettuccine. If your broccoli stems are tough, peel them first.

4 servings • 87 calories per serving

1½ cups	chopped broccoli (equal-size pieces)	360 ml
¼ cup	chicken stock	60 ml
2	cloves garlic, finely minced	
1 Tbs	chopped fresh parsley	15 ml
¾ cup	part-skim ricotta	180 ml
¼ cup	milk	60 ml
pinch	cayenne pepper or other ground red pepper	

Combine the broccoli, stock, garlic and parsley in a 9-inch (23-cm) glass pie dish and cover with vented plastic wrap. Microwave on full power until the broccoli is tender, 4½ to 5 minutes.

Drain the broccoli but don't lose the garlic or parsley. Then transfer to a processor or blender and whiz until smooth. With the motor running, add the ricotta, milk and cayenne or other red pepper and continue to whiz until you have a creamy sauce. Toss with hot pasta and serve.

Greek Tomato Sauce

If you can't find ripe, flavorful tomatoes, use canned, plum types instead. Serve with hot mostaccioli, ziti, rigatoni or in lasagna or moussaka.

Makes about 2 cups • 87 per ½-cup serving

1½ lb	plum tomatoes (about 12), peeled, seeded and chopped	675 g
2	cloves garlic, chopped	
2	scallions, chopped	
1 Tbs	olive oil	15 ml
1 tsp	lemon juice	5 ml
1 tsp	dillweed	5 ml
pinch	ground cinnamon	
	crumbled feta for tossing	

Combine all of the ingredients except the feta in a processor or blender and whiz until just combined. Scoop the mixture into a 9-inch (23-cm) glass pie dish and microwave, uncovered, on full power for 6 to 8 minutes, stopping to stir and rotate the dish a couple of times during cooking. Let the sauce stand for about 10 minutes before tossing with feta and hot pasta. The sauce (minus the feta) freezes well.

Pumpkin Seed Pesto

Toss with hot vermicelli or thin egg noodles.

4 servings • 217 calories per serving

¾ cup	green pumpkin seeds (pepitas)	180 ml
2	mild, green chili peppers, cored and seeded	
1	jalapeño pepper, cored and seeded (wear plastic gloves when handling)	
⅓ cup	fresh coriander	80 ml
⅔ cup	fresh, flat-leaf parsley	160 ml
pinch	ground cumin	
⅔ cup	beef stock	160 ml
1 Tbs	peanut oil	15 ml
	chopped black olives for sprinkling	
	freshly grated Parmesan for sprinkling	

Combine the pumpkin seeds, chilies, jalapeño, coriander, parsley, cumin, stock and oil in a processor or blender and whiz until you have a smooth paste.

Scoop the purree into a 9-inch (23-cm) glass pie dish and cover with vented plastic wrap. Microwave on full power until the pesto is thick and creamy, 3 to 4 minutes, stirring midway. Toss with hot pasta and sprinkle each serving with olives and Parmesan.

(continued)

Six Super Pasta Sauces–*Continued*

Mushroom and Pistachio Sauce

The darker the mushrooms, the more flavorful this sauce will be. Serve it hot or cold with fusilli, medium shells or cavatelli.

4 servings • 130 calories per serving

	olive oil for painting, if necessary	
2 cups	thinly sliced mushrooms	480 ml
2 Tbs	sweet butter	30 ml
2	scallions, finely minced	
⅓ cup	coarsely chopped pistachios	80 ml
	freshly grated Parmesan for sprinkling	
	minced fresh parsley for sprinkling	

Preheat a microwave browning dish according to manufacturer's directions, which will probably be about 4 minutes. Unless the dish has a nonstick surface, paint the hot dish with a bit of oil, add the mushrooms and microwave, uncovered, until the mushrooms are dark and fragrant, 1 to 2 minutes. If you don't have a browning dish, microwave the mushrooms in a 9-inch (23-cm) glass pie dish, uncovered, for 3 to 4 minutes. Let them stand while you prepare the rest of the sauce.

In a small bowl combine the butter, scallions and pistachios. Cover with vented plastic wrap and microwave on full power until the butter has melted, 1 to 2 minutes. Add the mushrooms, juice and all, toss with pasta and sprinkle with Parmesan and parsley.

Creamy Sweet Pepper Sauce

Serve with hot linguine, spaghetti or capellini. The sauce is also delicious with grilled salmon or bluefish.

4 servings • 35 calories per serving

3 Tbs	chicken stock	45 ml
3 Tbs	minced fresh chives	45 ml
2	cloves garlic, chopped	
1 tsp	rosemary	5 ml
1	bay leaf	
2	large sweet peppers, red or yellow, cored and chopped	
3 Tbs	light cream or milk	45 ml

Combine all of the ingredients except the cream or milk in a 9-inch (23-cm) glass pie dish. Cover with vented plastic wrap and microwave on full power until the peppers are tender, about 4 minutes, stirring or shaking midway. Let the mixture stand for about 2 minutes, then remove the bay leaf.

Scoop the mixture into a processor or blender and whiz until pureed and smooth, adding the cream or milk while the motor is running. Toss with hot pasta.

EGGPLANT STEAKS WITH BLACK BEAN SAUCE

Serve with snow peas (or thin green beans) and basmati or other aromatic rice.

4 servings • 104 calories per serving

2	cloves garlic, minced	
¼ tsp	cumin seeds, ground	1 ml
1 Tbs	peanut oil	15 ml
1	dried hot chili pepper	
1 Tbs	light soy sauce	15 ml
1½ tsp	honey	7 ml
1 Tbs	Chinese fermented black beans*, rinsed and chopped	15 ml
½ cup	chicken stock	120 ml
1	eggplant (about 1½ lb or 675 g)	
2 tsp	cornstarch	10 ml
splash	chili oil	
2 Tbs	chicken stock	30 ml
	minced scallions for sprinkling	

In a large, glass baking dish combine the garlic, cumin, peanut oil and chili. Cover with vented plastic wrap and microwave on full power until fragrant and the garlic is a bit tender, about 1 minute. Then add the soy sauce, honey, black beans, and ½ cup (120 ml) stock and combine well.

If the skin on the eggplant is tough, use a vegetable parer to slice away strips of the skin so that the eggplant appears striped. Slice the eggplant vertically into 4 steaks and bathe them on both sides in the black bean sauce. Then arrange the steaks so they're not overlapping, cover with vented plastic wrap and microwave on full power until tender, about 8 minutes. Flip the steaks midway.

Remove the eggplant steaks from the sauce and keep them warm. Then whisk the cornstarch, chili oil, and 2 Tbs (30 ml) stock into the black bean sauce. Cover and microwave on full power until slightly thickened, about 3 minutes. Pour over the steaks and sprinkle with scallions before serving.

*Available at Oriental markets.

FRESH EGG ROLLS

These aren't deep-fried, like the ones you may be used to. Instead the wrappers are made from rice flour and water and are called **Banh Trang, Gallettes de Riz** *or simply, rice paper. They are famous in many southeast Asian cuisines. They're available at Oriental markets and many supermarkets in clear, round or triangular packages. Rice paper has a faint basket weave pattern to it which comes from being dried on bamboo mats. The wrappers are thin, a bit fragile and sort of like handling filo dough.*

8	12-inch (35-cm) round rice papers	
2 cups	shredded nappa cabbage	480 ml
2 cups	mung, soy or other large, fresh bean sprouts	480 ml
1½ cups	thin green beans julienne	360 ml
5	scallions, minced	
2 Tbs	minced fresh mint	30 ml
2 Tbs	minced fresh basil	30 ml

4 servings • 76 calories per serving

It's best to microwave and assemble each roll, one by one, keeping finished rolls under a damp paper towel. First, wet a rice paper round under a bit of running water, set it on a plate, cover with vented plastic wrap and microwave on full power until tender, 25 to 30 seconds. Test this timing with your microwave because over-microwaving will make rice paper stiff and gummy and finally disintegrate it.

While the round is microwaving, combine the remaining ingredients in a large bowl. Scoop about ⅔ cup (160 ml) of the filling onto an edge of the rice paper and form it into a log with your hands. Fold the sides of the rice paper in, then roll up jelly roll style. Repeat with the remaining rice paper rounds and serve with Thai Dipping Sauce.

THAI DIPPING SAUCE

⅓ cup	chicken stock	80 ml
2 Tbs	*nam pla** or 1 Tbs light soy sauce	30 ml
1 Tbs	freshly squeezed lime juice	15 ml
1 Tbs	very finely minced sweet red peppers	15 ml

Combine all of the ingredients in a small bowl, cover with vented plastic wrap and microwave on full power until just warm and fragrant, about 1 minute. Use for dipping Fresh Egg Rolls, sliced poached chicken or steamed shrimp.

Nam pla is a dark, flavorful and pungent, fish-based sauce that's available in Oriental markets and specialty foods stores.

MARINATED TOFU

If you haven't tried it, microwaving is a simple and delicious way to enjoy tofu. Use either firm or soft tofu and serve as part of an Oriental feast.

2 servings • 88 calories per serving

½ lb	tofu (bean curd)	225 g
1 Tbs	orange juice	15 ml
1 Tbs	lemon juice	15 ml
splash	light soy sauce	
	sesame oil for sprinkling	
	minced scallions for sprinkling	
	toasted sesame seeds for sprinkling	

Cut the tofu in half so that you have two flattish rectangles. Then combine the juices and soy sauce in a 9-inch (23-cm) glass pie dish and add the tofu. Let the tofu marinate for about 10 minutes on each side. Then cover with vented plastic wrap and microwave on full power until the tofu is cooked through and fragrant, about 2½ minutes. Let stand for 2 minutes before sprinkling with sesame oil, scallions and sesame seeds. Serve warm.

PUMPKIN GNOCCHI WITH SWEET BUTTER AND PARMESAN

You may substitute sweet potato or winter squash for the pumpkin, but either way the gnocchi is nice with a side of broccoli.

4 servings • 207 calories per serving

1 lb	pumpkin, peeled and chopped into uniform pieces	450 g
¾ lb	white potatoes, peeled and chopped	340 g
2 Tbs	water	30 ml
2	eggs	
1 Tbs	whole wheat pastry flour	15 ml
¼ cup	ricotta	60 ml
¼ tsp	baking powder	1 ml
pinch	ground mace	
	olive oil for coating	
	melted sweet butter for sprinkling	
	freshly grated Parmesan for sprinkling	
	finely minced fresh chives for sprinkling	

Combine the pumpkin, potatoes and water in a 9-inch (23-cm) glass pie dish, cover with vented plastic wrap and micro-wave on full power until tender, 6 to 7 minutes. Stir or shake midway.

Scoop the pumpkin and potatoes into a processor or blender and whiz until smooth, adding the eggs, flour, ricotta, baking powder and mace while the motor is running. When smooth and well com-bined scoop into a bowl and chill for about 45 minutes.

Coat a large, round plate with a bit of oil. Then drop 8 tablespoons (soup spoons) of dough in a ring around the rim of the plate. Cover with vented plas-tic wrap and microwave on medium power until the gnocchi are slightly firm, 7 to 8 minutes, rotating the dish midway. Let stand while you complete the recipe with the remaining dough. You'll have about 24 gnocchi. Sprinkle with the butter, Parmesan and chives and serve warm.

SWEETS AND TREATS

We save up for them, calorie-wise. We stake out claims on our favorites, snatch tastes from other plates and ooh and ahh at them more than any other food we eat. Desserts are our gustatory rewards. They're celebratory, exceptional foods for the mere reason that we don't need them to survive. So in our hectic, no-time-to-spare world, desserts become important because they encourage us to relax, savor and feel a bit pampered. In other words, we may expect to have dinner at night, but a home-made dessert will have us wriggling in anticipation.

Microwaving delivers freshly made, delicious desserts in record time. And lucky for us, the best microwaved desserts are the most healthful. In this chapter you'll discover poached fruit and fruit sauces like Pear Fans in Mango Puree. Nutrients and colors are retained and the flavors are so bold you'll forget all about the whipped cream.

Puddings and custards can be microwaved deliciously with a minimum of fat because microwaving automatically keeps them silky. Crepes need no pan fat at all when microwaved because they don't stick. And granola can be microwaved with about one-sixth of the fat used otherwise.

Believe it or not, when homemade ice cream gets its start in the microwave, it becomes thicker and creamier without adding extra eggs or cream. That provides even more evidence that you can reduce fat and calories and become acquainted with delicious, healthful and imaginative desserts and treats.

One further point. Baked goods are not at their best made in the microwave. At the low end are the cakes, which can be heavy, spongy and so slippery that you need to rough up the surface with a serrated knife or the frosting will slide right off. Another problem with many of these cakes (pies and cookies, too) is that the flavors don't have time to mingle and each can be tasted separately in different parts of the mouth— egg, baking soda, sweetener and all. Valiant attempts have been made to cover up these unhomogenized tastes, and using aromatics like crystallized ginger helps, but the separate flavors creep out again in the aftertaste. For these reasons there will be no recipes for cakes, pies or cookies in this book.

Sweet Tips

Some of the puddings, custards and mousses in this chapter require the use of a microwave ring pan. The reason is that without one, microwaves will overcook the outside of the pudding before the center is cooked. Now I'm the first to admit that serving food in the shape of a ring pan is not always the most attractive choice. But use it anyway, then scoop the pudding into pretty dishes or goblets before serving and no one will ever know. Fresh mint leaves or citrus ribbons make nice decorations.

If you don't have a ring pan use a 9-inch (23-cm) glass pie dish and set a 2-inch (5-cm) juice glass upside down in the center of the pie dish.

FRUIT SALAD FROM KARIBA

The low-calorie dressing can also be used as a sauce for crepes or fresh berries.

4 servings • 111 calories per serving

In a small dish combine the lime juice, honey, cardamom, vanilla and butter. Microwave uncovered on full power until the butter has melted, about 40 seconds. Toss with the fruit and serve.

	juice and pulp of 1 lime	
1 tsp	honey	5 ml
	seeds of 1 cardamom pod, crushed	
1 or 2	drops of vanilla extract	
1 tsp	sweet butter	5 ml
4	fruits, like apples, pears, bananas, oranges, kiwifruit, or starfruit, sliced	

Honey Helper

Is your honey too firm to pour and measure? Microwave the glass or plastic jar on full power until it's liquid, 30 to 40 seconds for ½ cup (120 ml).

Vanilla Oil

Use a paring knife to slit a vanilla bean down the side. Add it to a small dish with ½ cup (120 ml) of peanut oil. Cover with vented plastic wrap and microwave on full power until warm and fragrant, 2½ to 3 minutes. Store in a tightly covered glass jar, bean and all.

Use vanilla oil to sauté fruit, on fruit salads and sweet dressings and in muffin and sweet bread recipes. In many recipes, especially fruit salad dressings, you'll need less oil because vanilla oil has more flavor.

CREAMY GRAPE DRESSING FOR FRUIT SALADS

Here's a rich and tasty dressing that's very low in fat and calories. The sweetness comes from the grapes, so choose them thoughtfully.

4 servings • 31 calories per serving

1 cup	seedless red grapes juice and pulp of ½ small lime	240 ml
¼ cup	vanilla yogurt	60 ml

Combine the grapes and lime juice in a processor or blender and whiz until smooth. Scoop into a small dish, cover with vented plastic wrap and microwave on full power until heated through and just bubbly, about 2 minutes. Let stand for about 5 minutes to cool, then fold in the yogurt.

Ideas for Using Creamy Grape Dressing

Toss with:

- Pear slices and almonds
- Orange sections
- Blueberries, crisp apple chunks and pecans
- Peach slices and strawberries
- Sliced fresh figs, minced dried apricots and toasted coconut

BLUEBERRY–ORANGE COULIS

When served with fresh fruit, it's a completely no-fat-added dessert.

4 servings • 35 calories per serving

1 cup	blueberries	240 ml
2 Tbs	freshly squeezed orange juice	30 ml
¼ tsp	freshly grated orange peel	1 ml
2 tsp	honey (if the berries aren't sweet)	10 ml

Combine all of the ingredients in a 9-inch (23-cm) glass pie dish. Cover with vented plastic wrap and microwave on full power until the berries are just soft, about 1½ minutes. Let stand for 1½ minutes, then scoop the mixture into a processor or blender and whiz until smooth.

Ideas for Using Blueberry-Orange Coulis

- Atop vanilla ice cream or plain, low-fat yogurt
- Atop a lemon mousse or cake
- Tossed with chilled tangerine sections
- Tossed with fresh strawberries or raspberries
- Drizzled over pancakes or crepes

STRAWBERRY-PEAR PUREE

This refreshing low-calorie sauce will keep for about a week, refrigerated. You may substitute blackberries for strawberries.

Makes about 1¼ cups • 11 calories per Tbs

2	large ripe pears, peeled, cored and sliced	
1 tsp	freshly squeezed lemon juice	5 ml
½ cup	fresh or unsweetened, frozen strawberries	120 ml
pinch	minced fresh ginger	

Arrange the pear slices in a 9-inch (23-cm) glass pie dish, add the lemon juice, cover with vented plastic wrap and microwave on full power until just tender, about 3 minutes.

Scoop the pears into a processor or blender and add the berries and ginger. Whiz until smooth and slightly fluffy.

Ideas for Using Strawberry-Pear Puree

- As a dip for apple or pear slices
- Tossed with sliced kiwi fruit and pitted fresh cherries
- As a sauce for poached pears, apples or waffles
- Mixed with an equal part of apple juice and served as a chilled dessert soup

PEAR FANS
IN MANGO PUREE

This is good with raspberries, too.

4 servings • 115 calories per serving

1	ripe mango
	juice and pulp of ½ lime
	juice and pulp of ½ orange
3	drops vanilla extract
3	pears, like red Bartlett
	fresh mint for garnishing, optional

Peel the mango over an open processor or blender and slice the flesh right in. Then turn the motor on, adding in the juices and vanilla and whiz until you have a smooth puree.

Scoop the puree into a 9-inch (23-cm) glass pie dish. Then halve the pears vertically and make vertical cuts in each half (don't cut through the stem end) to make little fans.

Arrange the pears in the dish, flat side down, fat part toward the outside. Cover with vented plastic wrap and microwave on full power for 6 to 8 minutes. Let stand 5 minutes.

Serve in flat, glass dessert dishes. First pour in the puree, then set in 1 or 2 pear halves and garnish with the mint if desired.

PEARS AND PLANTAINS

Plantains are high-fiber, large cooking bananas from the tropics. For this recipe choose ones with black skins and creamy pale flesh.

4 servings • 144 calories per serving

1 Tbs	maple syrup	15 ml
1 tsp	orange juice concentrate	5 ml
2 tsp	sweet butter	10 ml
2 Tbs	apple juice	30 ml
pinch	freshly ground allspice	
2	pears, cored and cut into equal-size chunks	
2	plantains, peeled and sliced into equal-size coins	
	crushed roasted peanuts for sprinkling	

In a 9-inch (23-cm) glass pie dish combine the maple syrup, concentrate, butter, apple juice and allspice. Cover with vented plastic wrap and microwave on full power until the butter has melted, about 30 seconds.

Add the pears and plantains to the dish, cover and microwave on full power until tender, about 3 minutes, stirring or shaking every minute.

Let stand for 2 minutes, sprinkle with the peanuts and serve.

GLAZED FRESH PEACHES WITH APRICOT PRESERVE

4 servings • 93 calories per serving

2 Tbs	freshly squeezed lemon juice	30 ml
1 Tbs	maple syrup	15 ml
2 Tbs	apricot preserve	30 ml
pinch	freshly grated nutmeg	
4	fresh peaches, peeled, halved and pitted	
	toasted slivered almonds for sprinkling	

To make the glaze, in a small bowl combine the lemon juice, maple syrup, preserve and nutmeg. Cover with vented plastic wrap and microwave on full power until bubbly, about 40 seconds.

Meanwhile, arrange the peaches, flat side down, in a 9-inch (23-cm) glass pie dish and spoon the glaze over them so they're coated and shiny. Cover with vented plastic wrap and microwave on full power until heated through and slightly soft, about 2½ minutes. Let stand for 2 minutes.

To serve, set the peach halves, flat side down, on dessert plates, drizzle some glaze on each and sprinkle with the almonds.

Note: The peaches are also great atop vanilla ice cream and if you have extra glaze, enjoy it with vanilla yogurt or pudding.

ORANGE-CARAMEL POPCORN

Here's a way to take fat and calories (but not flavor) out of a traditional treat.

4 servings • 187 calories per serving

2 Tbs	sweet butter	30 ml
1 tsp	finely minced fresh orange peel	5 ml
¼ cup	maple syrup	60 ml
¼ tsp	ground cinnamon	1 ml
¼ cup	cashew pieces	60 ml
6 cups	popcorn	1½ liters

Melt the butter in a 9-inch (23-cm) glass pie dish. Then add the orange peel, maple syrup and cinnamon and microwave, uncovered, on full power until bubbly. When it just begins to turn color (1½ to 3½ minutes), it's done.

Meanwhile, have the cashew pieces and popcorn ready in a huge bowl. Pour on the caramel and be careful, it is hot. With a large rubber spatula, toss quickly and well to coat and let stand for about 20 minutes before serving.

RICE PUDDING WITH CARDAMOM AND ALMONDS

Microwaving keeps the texture smooth and creamy without lots of extra eggs—good news if you're watching cholesterol.

Be sure the rice is at room temperature. If it's hot, the pudding will come out starchy.

6 servings • 250 calories per serving

3 cups	cooked rice	720 ml
1½ cups	milk, skim milk or light cream	360 ml
2	eggs, beaten	
	seeds from 3 cardamom pods, ground	
splash	almond extract	
¼ tsp	vanilla extract	1 ml
⅓ cup	honey	80 ml
2	drops orange flower water, optional	
pinch	freshly grated nutmeg	
	slivered almonds for sprinkling	

Scoop the rice into a 7-inch (18-cm) microwave-safe ring pan.

Then whisk together the milk or cream, eggs, cardamom, extracts, honey, orange flower water and nutmeg and pour it over the rice.

Microwave, uncovered, on full power until firm but a bit jiggly, 7½ to 8 minutes, stirring every 2 minutes. Let stand for about 5 minutes. When you're ready to serve, scoop the pudding into pretty dishes and sprinkle with the almonds. Serve warm or chilled.

CHEESECAKE MOUSSE WITH RASPBERRY-LEMON GLAZE

Nice with sliced papaya on the side.

6 servings • 220 calories per serving

1 cup	neufchâtel or cream cheese	240 ml
½ cup	vanilla yogurt	120 ml
2	eggs, beaten	
	juice of ½ lemon	
1 tsp	vanilla extract	5 ml
¼ cup	maple syrup	60 ml
pinch	freshly grated nutmeg	
1 Tbs	whole wheat pastry flour	15 ml
¼ cup	raspberry jam	60 ml
¼ tsp	grated fresh lemon peel	1 ml

Use a hand mixer on medium speed to combine the cheese, yogurt, eggs, lemon juice, vanilla, maple syrup, nutmeg and flour. Don't overmix, keep it thick. When it's well combined, scoop into a 7-inch (18-cm) microwave-safe ring pan and microwave, uncovered, on medium power until the mousse just begins to move away from the sides of the pan and a knife comes out clean, 7 to 8 minutes. Let the mousse stand while you prepare the glaze.

In a small dish combine the jam and lemon peel. Cover with vented plastic wrap and microwave on full power until bubbly, about 1 minute.

Drizzle over the mousse and roll the pan around so the top is completely coated. Chill for about 3 hours. Cut into slices and serve.

PEACH BREAD PUDDING WITH PECANS

A high-fiber dessert, snack or breakfast. Serve with sliced fresh peaches.

4 servings • 287 calories per serving

¾ cup	milk	180 ml
1 Tbs	cornstarch	15 ml
7	slices whole wheat bread, cut into equal-size cubes	
⅓ cup	peach jam	80 ml
1	egg, beaten	
1 tsp	vanilla extract	5 ml
	pecans for sprinkling	
	sweet butter for dotting	

Stir together the milk and cornstarch in a large measuring cup and microwave, uncovered, on full power until thick and bubbly, about 2 minutes, stirring midway.

Toss the bread cubes into a 1-quart (1-liter) casserole dish. When the milk is ready, whisk in the jam, egg and vanilla and pour over the bread. Sprinkle with pecans and dot with a bit of butter. Then microwave, uncovered, on medium power until cooked through and bubbly around the sides, about 8 minutes. Let stand for about 10 minutes before serving warm.

Easier Shelling

To shell 1 cup (240 ml) of pecans or other nuts, toss with 3 tablespoons (45 ml) of water in a 9-inch (23-cm) glass pie dish. Cover with vented plastic wrap and microwave on full power for about 2 minutes. Then drain and let stand until cool enough to handle and shell.

PUMPKIN CUSTARD

Microwaving the milk first encourages a creamy texture, without using cream.

4 servings • 129 calories per serving

1 cup	milk	240 ml
2 tsp	cornstarch	10 ml
1	egg, beaten	
1 tsp	vanilla extract	5 ml
⅔ cup	pumpkin puree	160 ml
¼ cup	maple syrup	60 ml
¼ tsp	ground mace	1 ml
¼ tsp	ground cinnamon	1 ml

Whisk the milk and cornstarch together in a glass measuring cup. Microwave on full power until hot but not boiling, about 1 minute. Stir and set aside.

Meanwhile, whisk together the egg, vanilla, pumpkin, maple syrup, mace and cinnamon. Let the milk cool a bit before you whisk it in.

Pour the mixture into a large bowl and set it right on the microwave floor. Microwave, uncovered, on medium power until firm, 7 to 8 minutes, stirring every 2 minutes.

Scoop the custard into pretty dessert dishes and chill for about an hour before serving. Coconut Sprinkles (below) make a nice decoration.

Coconut Sprinkles

These are nice on Pumpkin Custard (above) and other creamy desserts. Spread out 3 tablespoons (45 ml) grated unsweetened coconut on a double thickness of paper towels. Microwave, uncovered, on full power until dry and crisp but not burned, about 8 minutes, tossing every 2 minutes. It tastes chewy, crunchy and candied, without sugar. Store tightly sealed.

ORANGE-ALMOND CUSTARD

Good news if you're watching fat and calories—skim milk works in this recipe.

4 servings • 143 calories per serving

1 cup	milk	240 ml
1 Tbs	cornstarch	15 ml
2	eggs	
¼ tsp	almond extract	1 ml
1 tsp	vanilla extract	5 ml
3 Tbs	maple syrup	45 ml
splash	orange extract	
	slivered toasted almonds for sprinkling	

Whisk together the milk and cornstarch in a large measuring cup and microwave, uncovered, on full power until just thickened, about 3 minutes, whisking each minute.

Meanwhile beat the eggs until they are thick and a lemony color. Then beat in the almond and vanilla extracts, maple syrup and orange extract.

Next beat in a little hot milk and continue beating while you slowly add the rest of the milk. If there are bubbles, let them die down.

Pour the mixture into 4 cups or ramekins and set them right on the microwave floor. Microwave, uncovered, on medium power until firm but a bit jiggly, 5 to 6 minutes. Let stand for 5 minutes, then sprinkle with the almonds and serve immediately.

AFRICAN CORN AND PEANUT PUDDING

Pureed corn sweetens and thickens without a lot of calories and fat.

4 servings • 170 calories per serving

Puree the corn in a processor or blender and add in the milk, coconut, cornstarch, maple syrup, vanilla, allspice and ginger while the motor is running.

Pour into a 9-inch (23-cm) glass pie dish and microwave, uncovered, on full power until bubbly, 2½ to 3 minutes. Then whisk robustly and microwave until thick, about 1 minute more.

⅔ cup	cooked corn kernels	160 ml
1 cup	milk	240 ml
¼ cup	grated unsweetened coconut	60 ml
3 Tbs	cornstarch	45 ml
¼ cup	maple syrup	60 ml
1 tsp	vanilla extract	5 ml
¼ tsp	ground allspice	1 ml
¼ tsp	ground ginger	1 ml
2 Tbs	chopped toasted peanuts	30 ml

Scoop into wine goblets or pretty dessert bowls, sprinkle with the peanuts and serve warm.

APRICOT SNACK BARS

Great for breakfast, snacks and dessert with peanut butter, apricot jam or orange marmalade.

Makes 16 little bars • 112 calories per bar

Scoop the apricots, raisins and pecans into a processor or blender and whiz until finely chopped. Then set them aside for later.

Combine the juices, maple syrup and butter in a small dish, cover with vented plastic wrap and microwave on full power until the butter has melted, about 2 minutes.

In a large bowl combine the oats, corn-meal, flour, cream of tartar, nutmeg, ginger, cinnamon and baking soda. Add in the apricot mixture, then use a large rubber spatula to stir in the juice mixture. Continue to stir while you add in the egg.

When the batter is completely combined, scoop it into a 7-inch (18-cm) microwave-safe ring pan and level out the top with the spatula. Microwave, uncovered, until cooked through and the

1¼	cups	dried apricots	300 ml
¾	cup	raisins	180 ml
¼	cup	pecans	60 ml
¼	cup	white grape juice	60 ml
¼	cup	orange juice	60 ml
2	Tbs	maple syrup	30 ml
1	Tbs	sweet butter	15 ml
1	cup	rolled oats	240 ml
¼	cup	cornmeal	60 ml
¼	cup	whole wheat pastry flour	60 ml
	pinch	cream of tartar	
¼	tsp	freshly grated nutmeg	1 ml
¼	tsp	ground ginger	1 ml
¼	tsp	ground cinnamon	1 ml
½	tsp	baking soda	2 ml
1		egg, beaten	

sides of the dough have moved away from the pan, about 8 minutes, rotating the pan midway.

Let stand on a wire rack for about 20 minutes, then slice into bars and serve.

Note: Wrap the bars tightly if you're going to save them, but they're best eaten the same day. The small amount of fat won't keep them moist forever.

EDIBLE CUPS FOR SWEETS (TUILES)

You may serve mousse, pudding or other desserts in these little edible cups called **tuiles** *(too–EEZ). Traditionally they are made with almond meal and lots of butter. Thanks to the microwave, this version is greatly reduced in fat and calories.*

1 Tbs	sweet butter	15 ml
2 Tbs	maple syrup	30 ml
½ cup plus 1 Tbs	rolled oats	135 ml
2 Tbs	whole wheat pastry flour	30 ml
pinch	ground cinnamon	
1	egg, beaten	

Makes 4 edible cups • 128 calories each

In a small dish, melt the butter on full power. Then stir in the maple syrup, oats, flour, cinnamon and egg. Work quickly and don't let the batter stand around or the oats could absorb too much liquid, making the *tuiles* gummy.

In a custard cup or ramekin that has been sprayed with vegetable cooking spray, spread ¼ of the batter evenly on bottom and partially up sides. Microwave on full power until firm, 1 to 1½ minutes. Unmold immediately. Repeat the process with the remaining batter.

Let the *tuiles* cool until firm and crisp; overnight may be necessary in very humid weather.

Ideas for Using Tuiles

Fill with:
- Berries
- Fruit compote
- Flavored yogurt
- African Corn and Peanut Pudding (page 236)
- Peach Filling for a Tart or Pie (page 248)
- Vanilla ice cream

FROZEN LIME AND HONEY MOUSSE

This mousse contains no refined sugar but the extra gelatin helps keep the texture soft in the freezer. For best results, serve the mousse the day it is prepared.

4 servings • 207 calories per serving

1½ Tbs	unflavored gelatin		22 ml
½ cup	white grape juice		120 ml
	juice and pulp of 4 limes		
⅓ cup	honey		80 ml
2	egg yolks, beaten		
1 cup	milk		240 ml
2	egg whites, beaten to soft peaks		

Combine the gelatin and grape juice in a large measuring cup and microwave on full power, uncovered, until the gelatin has dissolved, about 1½ minutes. It could take longer if the juice is cold.

In a large bowl whisk together the dissolved gelatin, lime juice, honey, yolks and milk. Continue to whisk while you add in the egg whites.

Pour the mixture into a shallow dish and set into the freezer. Whisk every 10 minutes or so until the mixture begins to thicken, about 45 mintues. This step is important.

Continue to freeze for 2 to 3 hours more, then scoop into pretty bowls and serve.

DRIED FRUIT COMPOTE

4 servings • 283 calories per serving

16 oz	dried fruit, like peaches,	450 g
	apricots, prunes and figs	
	juice and pulp of 1 lemon	
	juice and pulp of 1 lime	
2	drops almond extract	
	lime peel ribbons for	
	garnishing	

Combine the fruit, juices and almond extract in a 9-inch (23-cm) glass pie dish. Cover with vented plastic wrap and microwave on full power until the fruit just begins to plump, about 4½ minutes, stirring or shaking midway.

Let stand for 4 minutes, then serve warm or chilled garnished with the lime ribbons.

For a Change of Taste

- Serve in Edible Cups for Sweets *(Tuiles),* page 238

- Serve atop vanilla yogurt, ice cream or a slice of cake
- Spoon over steaming oatmeal for breakfast
- Use to fill tiny tart shells
- Serve over a chunk of brie
- Use as a garnish for grilled chicken

Plumped Dried Fruit

To plump dried fruit, like raisins, toss ½ cup (120 ml) in a small bowl and cover with 2 tablespoons (30 ml) of orange juice. Cover with vented plastic wrap and microwave on full power until the fruit has absorbed the juice, about 2 minutes. Let stand for 2 minutes, then sprinkle on yogurt, cereals or fruit salads.

DESSERT CREPES

Here's an opportunity to enjoy crepes without having to grease the pan.

Makes 4 or 5 large crepes • 64 calories per crepe

2	eggs, beaten	
¼ cup	milk	60 ml
1 Tbs	whole wheat pastry flour	15 ml
2 tsp	maple syrup	10 ml
¼ tsp	vanilla extract	1 ml
pinch	freshly grated nutmeg	

In a large bowl whisk together all of the ingredients.

Spray a 5- to 6-inch (12- to 15-cm) round dish with vegetable cooking spray and pour in about 3 Tbs (45 ml) of batter. Microwave, uncovered, on medium power until the crepe is cooked, about 2 minutes. Flip face side down on waxed paper, loosening crepe with a butter knife if necessary, and repeat with the remaining batter.

If you don't have a 5- to 6-inch (12- to 15-cm) round dish, use the closest size you've got. Pour in the batter and roll it around until you've made a 5- to 6-inch (12- to 15-cm) crepe. Be careful that the batter doesn't run past 6 inches (15 cm).

Ideas for Tasty Fillings

- Spread with neufchâtel or cream cheese, sprinkle with sliced seedless grapes and roll
- Set a chunk of brie and a pear slice in the middle and fold into a bundle, then microwave on low power until the brie is soft
- Fold into fans and cover with a splash each of orange and lemon juice, then microwave until just warm and serve with fresh fruit
- Fill with pudding or ice cream
- Fill with sliced peaches and toasted pecans
- Fill with raspberries and vanilla yogurt
- Spread with orange marmalade, sprinkle with blueberries and roll
- Spread with currant jelly, sprinkle with toasted almonds and chopped figs and roll

WARM CITRUS COMPOTE

A good source of vitamin C—a wonderful winter treat.

4 servings • 93 calories per serving

Combine the grapefruit and tangerine sections in a 9-inch (23-cm) glass pie dish along with the lime juice and maple syrup. If the sections are a bit tart you'll need more maple syrup.

Cover with vented plastic wrap and microwave on full power until warm and fragrant, about 4 minutes, stirring or shaking midway. Let stand for a couple of minutes.

Serve warm, sprinkled with the pecans.

2	grapefruits, pink or white, sectioned with pith removed	
2	tangerines, sectioned with pith removed	
1 Tbs	freshly squeezed lime juice	15 ml
1 Tbs	maple syrup, or to taste	15 ml
	chopped pecans for sprinkling	

Serving Ideas

- In pretty crystal bowls or wine goblets
- In grapefruit halves
- In or over crepes
- Atop waffles for dessert or breakfast

CRUNCHY CANDIED NUTS

These remind me of the delicious and famous Chinese deep-fried nuts. This version has absolutely no added fat.

Makes about a cup • 214 calories per ¼-cup serving

1	egg white, beaten to stiff peaks	
1 Tbs plus 1 tsp	maple syrup	20 ml
1 tsp	orange juice	5 ml
½ tsp	ground cinnamon	2 ml
pinch	ground ginger	
pinch	curry powder	
1 cup	walnut halves	240 ml

Measure all of the ingredients into a medium bowl and combine well so that all the nuts are coated.

Set a sheet of waxed paper on a dinner plate and arrange the nuts in a ring around the rim. Microwave, uncovered, on medium power until dry to the touch, 8½ to 9 minutes, stirring midway.

Let the nuts stand until cool on a fresh sheet of waxed paper.

Variation: Pecans are delicious, too, and will only require 7 to 7½ minutes of microwaving.

Flavored Honeys

Honeys flavored with orange, lemon, vanilla or cinnamon can be used in baking, in fruit salad dressings, in fruit sauces or by themselves drizzled over a just-baked muffin.

To flavor 1 cup (240 ml) of honey, pour it into a small bowl and add your choice of flavoring. A long ribbon of citrus peel, a vanilla bean or a cinnamon stick are some ideas. Then cover with vented plastic wrap and microwave on full power until very liquidy and fragrant, about 3 minutes. Let cool, then store, flavoring and all, well covered.

ALMOND FRUIT BARS

High in fiber and flavor.

Makes about 16 bars • 72 calories per bar

1 cup	pitted prunes	240 ml
¼ cup	raisins	60 ml
¼ cup	almonds	60 ml
½ cup	rolled oats	120 ml
⅓ cup	whole wheat pastry flour	80 ml
¼ tsp	ground cinnamon	1 ml
¼ tsp	freshly ground nutmeg	1 ml
¼ tsp	ground ginger	1 ml
1 tsp	vanilla extract	5 ml
2	eggs, beaten	

Toss the prunes and raisins into a processor or blender and whiz until finely chopped. Pour into a large bowl along with the almonds, oats, flour, cinnamon, nutmeg, ginger, vanilla and eggs. It's easier to mix the batter with your hands.

When the batter is well combined, press it into a 7-inch (18-cm) microwave-safe ring pan. Make sure the top is level. Microwave, uncovered, on full power until cooked through and the dough has moved away from the sides of the pan, about 5 minutes, rotating the pan midway.

Let the pan cool on a wire rack for about 15 minutes, then slice and serve.

APPLES OR PEARS WITH CARAMEL SAUCE

A famous autumn treat, but without refined sugar and excess fat. This recipe is especially nice when served over vanilla ice cream, cake or vanilla yogurt.

4 servings • 166 calories per serving

1½ Tbs	sweet butter	22 ml
2½ Tbs	maple syrup	38 ml
pinch	ground cinnamon	
½ tsp	vanilla extract	2 ml
4	apples or pears, cored and sliced	
2 Tbs	grated unsweetened coconut	30 ml
1 Tbs	finely ground pecans	15 ml

In a small bowl melt the butter on full power for about 1½ minutes. Then stir in the maple syrup, cinnamon and vanilla and microwave, uncovered, on full power until bubbly, 1½ to 3 minutes. Don't let the caramel turn brown or it will taste burnt.

Meanwhile, pat the fruit slices dry with paper towels and toss them into a large bowl with the coconut and pecans. When the caramel sauce is ready, use a rubber spatula to scoop it over the fruit mixture and toss until it's completely coated.

Let stand for about 3 minutes before serving warm.

IN BANANA HEAVEN

Bananas are an excellent source of potassium.

4 servings • 162 calories per serving

	juice of 1 orange	
1 Tbs	maple syrup	15 ml
2 tsp	sweet butter	10 ml
pinch	ground cinnamon	
4	bananas, sliced into spears	
	chopped macadamia nuts for sprinkling	

Combine the juice, maple syrup, butter and cinnamon in a 9-inch (23-cm) glass pie dish. Cover with vented plastic wrap and microwave on full power until the butter has melted, about 1½ minutes.

When the butter has melted, add the bananas to the dish and toss well. Cover and continue to microwave on full power until the bananas are just tender, about 4 minutes. Serve warm sprinkled with the macadamia nuts.

Ideas for Better Bananas

- Atop pancakes
- In ice cream cones
- In parfait glasses, layered with vanilla yogurt or ice cream

Variation: To be in pineapple heaven, substitute fresh pineapple spears for the bananas. Half pineapple and half banana is nice, too.

MAPLE VANILLA ICE CREAM (OR ICE MILK)

Microwaving and prechilling the ice cream base encourages a creamier texture and more volume without the addition of extra eggs and cream. Skim milk may be used also, but the texture won't be as alluring.

3 cups	cream or milk, or some of each	720 ml
1	egg	
½ cup	maple syrup	120 ml
2 tsp	vanilla extract	10 ml

Makes about a quart • 238 calories per ½-cup serving

Beat half of the cream and/or milk together with the egg and microwave, uncovered, on medium power until slightly thickened, about 5 minutes. The cream, at this point, should coat the back of a spoon.

Let the cream cool, then whisk in the remaining cream and/or milk, maple syrup and vanilla and chill overnight.

Process in an ice cream maker according to manufacturer's directions.

Added Attractions

After the ice cream is processed, you may want to add:

- Chopped pecans
- Chocolate chips
- Crushed cookies
- Coconut Sprinkles (page 234)

PEACH FILLING FOR A TART OR PIE

Makes enough for 1 tart or pie
(8 servings) • 195 calories per serving

4 cups	peeled, sliced peaches	1 liter
⅓ cup	chopped, dried apricots	80 ml
3 Tbs	maple syrup, or to taste	45 ml
pinch	freshly ground allspice	
pinch	freshly grated nutmeg	
1 tsp	freshly squeezed lime juice	5 ml
¼ cup	whole wheat pastry flour	60 ml
1	9-inch (23-cm) baked tart or thin pie shell	

Combine the peaches, apricots, maple syrup, allspice, nutmeg, lime juice and flour in a large bowl and toss well to combine. If the peaches are a bit tart you'll need more maple syrup.

Scoop the peach mixture into a 9-inch (23-cm) glass pie dish and microwave, uncovered, on full power until thick and bubbly, 4½ to 5 minutes, stirring a couple of times during microwaving. Let stand for about 4 minutes, then scoop into the baked shell and chill until firm.

Variations:

- If you like, you can spread pastry cream in the bottom of the shell before adding the peaches.
- For a tasty, lower-calorie idea, paint the shell with raspberry jam, then add the peaches.
- Frozen peaches can be used, but you'll need more flour, about ⅓ cup (80 ml) total.

Apple Appeal

Scoop out the core of a McIntosh or other nice cooking apple. Then wrap it in plastic wrap and poke it clear through the skin with a skewer about 12 times. Microwave on full power until tender, about 3 minutes. Use rubber gloves to remove the plastic wrap, fill the core with grated cheddar, minced raisins and walnuts and let the apple stand for 2 minutes. Great for a quick breakfast, snack or dessert.

RAISIN-OAT GRANOLA

Enjoy for breakfast, snacks or sprinkled over fruit for dessert. Compared to other granolas, this is very low in fat.

Makes about 2½ cups • 130 calories per ¼-cup serving

2 tsp	sweet butter	10 ml
¼ cup	maple syrup	60 ml
¼ tsp	ground cinnamon	1 ml
½ tsp	vanilla extract	2 ml
2 cups	rolled oats	480 ml
¼ cup	chopped pecans	60 ml
½ cup	raisins	120 ml

In a small bowl combine the butter, maple syrup and cinnamon. Microwave, uncovered, on full power until the butter has melted, about 1½ minutes. Then add the vanilla.

In a large bowl combine the oats and pecans. Pour on the butter mixture and use a large rubber spatula to mix well until all the oats are coated.

Line the bottom of the microwave with waxed paper and spread out the granola. Microwave on full power until the granola is dry, 3½ to 4 minutes, stirring midway.

Add the raisins and let stand for about 3 minutes before serving. If there's any left, store it very tightly covered.

COOL RASPBERRY AND RHUBARB SAUCE

Serve over fresh fruit chunks, cake, frozen yogurt or ice cream.

Makes about 1⅔ cups • 4 calories per Tbs

1½ cups	chopped tender rhubarb	360	ml
¼ cup	maple syrup, or to taste	60	ml
1	orange, seeded and sectioned		
½ cup	red raspberries	120	ml
½ cup	vanilla yogurt	120	ml

In a 9-inch (23-cm) glass pie dish combine the rhubarb, maple syrup and orange sections. If the rhubarb is very tart you may need more maple syrup. Cover with vented plastic wrap and microwave on full power until the rhubarb is tender, 5½ to 6 minutes, stirring or shaking midway. Let stand about 3 minutes.

Scoop the rhubarb mixture into a processor or blender and whiz until smooth, adding the raspberries while the motor is running. Refrigerate the sauce and when it's cool, fold in the yogurt.

Note: To rid the raspberries of their seeds, press them through a fine mesh strainer before adding them to the processor. If the seeds don't bother you, leave them in, they're a good source of dietary fiber.

INDEX

Page numbers in italics indicate illustrations and charts.